Dedicated to my eldest daughter Caroline, who urged me to write it.
It was due to her persistence that I finally put pen to paper.
Thank you Caroline.

# Bite the Bullet, Bootsie!

## You're an Isle of Wighter

## By
## Bootsie Bettenson

Book design by: Sue Matthews

Printed in the United Kingdom

First Printing, 2021

ISBN: 978-1-7398098-0-5 (Paperback)
ISBN: 978-1-7398098-1-2 (eBook)

Published by Bootsie's Books
Ryde, Isle of Wight PO33 3QQ

# Bite the Bullet, Bootsie!

## You're an Isle of Wighter

## Foreword

I'd like to thank my eldest daughter Caroline for her encouragement to finally write this book.

Also, the people who showed me how to accomplish the skills required to do not just heavy duty engineering but also the light engineering of J.S.Whites, and GKN respectively.

Thanks also to Betto, Arthur Kilmartin, Ray Thomas, my primary school teacher Mr. O'Neil, Mrs Corbin in the grammar school, and of course my long-suffering wife, for putting up with me all these years, fast approaching 60 years together – I still love her to bits.

I trust this will be as enjoyable for you, dear reader, as it was for me to put pen to paper.

And may God bless you,


Bootsie Bettenson

# Chapter 1

## *Island Beginnings*

This is a true account of my life-story. For many years I've wanted to write a book about it, because I happen to be one of those characters in life that things 'happen' to. My sense of humour, and also my big mouth, have got me into more trouble than enough, on many occasions.

Mostly, however, a ready wit, and quick talking, have got me out of the trouble in most cases.

I was a 'War Baby', a term that would unsettle me for all of my formative years. I felt the deep shame and insignificance that the stigma of my illegitimacy had brought me.

I was born on New Year's Day 1943. I didn't ask to be born, did I? We just have to get on with our lives, don't we, eh?

In Louis Road, Lake, where my mother and grandfather lived, was billeted a company of soldiers. They were destined to fight for King and Country, in the second World War. One of those soldiers decided to take by force, sexual gratification from a woman against her will. That was my mother. He had attacked her.

When my mother began to show the obvious signs of her pregnancy, the shock, I believe, brought on a massive heart attack for my maternal grandmother. She died – just 42 years of age. But tragedy was to strike once more, when my mother was six months pregnant.

Gordon, her husband, was one of the proverbial 'Desert Rats' under Montgomery. He was due to come home on leave three months before I was due to be born! What a sight to greet him would that have been to see his wife, with child, from another man.

However, the troopship he was on was sunk with all hands, by a German 'U' boat. A family of four was now a family of two.

I have a postcard of Gordon, which was sent to my mother before his leave was confirmed. He was a very handsome young man, with curly hair. He was standing in front of a tent in the desert, wearing a khaki shirt and shorts, with a beautiful smile upon his face. I only wish to God he could have been my father, but it wasn't to be, was it.

The card was a virtual love letter to my mum, perhaps the last piece of correspondence she was to receive.

When I was eventually born, in St Mary's Hospital, Newport, I was abandoned there, in the old part of the hospital – namely, what used to be known as the 'Workhouse'.

I became a reject, disowned for two years. That, dear ones, was war at the sharp end, so to speak. I was destined to become a Bevan Boy who would work down the mines, perhaps in the Rhonda Valley, or a Dr Barnardo's Boy.

I knew very little about my maternal grandmother. She had an Irish surname. Her name was Kathleen Louisa, affectionately referred to as 'Kitty', by grandad. Delving into her background and by comments made on 'FaceBook', her forbears were possibly Polish refugees – who settled in a place called Dungannon, on the North West coast of Eire.

Photographs of her? Not one, as my grandfather's second wife saw to it that they were destroyed. One year after Kitty's death, my grandpa remarried. He neglected (deliberately) to mention to his second wife-to-be, the existence of his grandson.

A year later (by this time I was two years old), Nana, my surrogate grandmother found out about my existence. The fat then hit the fan, as the saying goes. Because of my mother and her father's deception, Nana came to a decision that was to change my entire life. There was never any doubt in my mind 'who wore the trousers', as the saying goes. Nana was only about 5ft 1in, maybe 5ft 2in, but you would cross her at your peril.

In no uncertain terms, she shouted at my grandfather, "Fred – you and I are going to bring up your Grandson," and they did. True to her word, she applied for, and got, custody of me.

She originated from a place called 'Rudmore Square, Portsmouth'. She didn't want to get on with my mother so she and grandad sold up their house in Louis Road, Lake – to move to Lake Road, Portsmouth. They bought a café, called the Cosy Café, but it was anything but cosy.

Let me explain. I was about five years old at the time - life was certainly different when the soldiers and sailors were under the same roof, in that small café.

One or two ringleaders from either side would goad the opposing soldiers into some form of action, usually ending in a free for all. I can still remember, although only five and half to six years old, the meals ending up on the floor of the café, the crockery being smashed, the tables being overturned as the fighting ensued. It was a regular occurrence.

You see, these men were going to war. They were intent on letting off steam. This place called Portsmouth was a major stepping off point, before the servicemen were shipped abroad, possibly to the front line.

At least once a month there would be a 'battle royal' going on at the 'Cosy Café'. When battle commenced, my grandfather would phone the hotline to the M.Ps (Military Police). Within five or six minutes you'd see two military policemen arrive on the scene.

The response from the servicemen was extraordinary. Immediately, the fist fighting stopped. Two 6ft 3" M.Ps, built like brick built outhouses, suddenly had the respect which wasn't shown to my Nana and her husband.

'What's the damage, guv?' they would ask. And then, they would make the squaddies or matelots, cough up the ready money to pay the bills for the trouble they'd caused.

Before I continue Life's journey over Portsmouth, there are three incidents I would like to share with you.

First, I could get myself into trouble, without even trying. For example, the week-old chicks my Grandfather would purchase. In Louis Road, Lake we had a reasonably large garden and we kept chickens. The reason was twofold. Firstly, they supplied us with eggs, and secondly, after giving of their best in the egg-laying stakes, the birds could become the source of supply for Christmas Dinner. Supply and demand meant that they were a suitable form of investment.

One day, I surveyed, at the tender age of 4, what I thought was a problem. Now the week-old chicks were kept separate from the rest of the chickens in a small chicken coop, which kept them warm and safe. For some inexplicable reason, I felt they needed a bit more freedom, so I lifted the wooden flap that separated them from the older birds allowing them freedom I felt they needed.

Unfortunately, the chickens that they were segregated from had other ideas and began to attack the baby chicks. I quickly rushed round to the side of the chicken run, and digging the soil out to lift the chicken wire, began to free the little chicks. Into where? The rest of the garden. It took for ages to round up these small birds – I got a good old cut across the calf of my legs for my troubles, a copper stick being the weapon used. Even at this tender age I knew I deserved the punishment. Chè sera, sera – what will be, will be.

This serves to illustrate how strong-willed I was. If I wanted something, I would 'go for it', as the saying goes. I can be very obstinate, and I can still remember my 'temper tantrum' when I didn't always get my own way.

The chicken saga was incident number one. The second incident – nearly being run over by a double-decker bus.

Now, Queenie White was looking after me, when I suddenly 'took off' down the road, towards the junction of Louis Road and Newport Road. To me, it was a game but for Queenie? She had to get her skates on. She grabbed me around the middle, just as I was about to step off the pavement. She saved my life!

Incident number three – My Nana went to court, and with my grandfather in tow, applied for and became my guardians. As guardians, my mother Amy had little say in how I was to be brought up. My stepgran absolutely hated my mother. I can remember both women literally fighting and pulling one another's hair out, such was the animosity they bore to one another.

One morning, very early, my mum decided to do a 'runner' taking me with her. She had got a job as a live-in housekeeper at Ventnor. Apparently, the man she was to work for, another Gordon, had a daughter called Pat. He was a widower and had a young girl to bring up. He had to work to put food on the table, so to speak, hence the need for his daughter to be looked after, allowing him the freedom to work for his living. His daughter, as far as I can remember, was about seven or eight years old.

As I had gone missing, I was made a Ward of Court. The police eventually tracked me down, and I was returned back to my Nana's care. I say 'Nana's care' because my grandfather had very little input into my upbringing. He was quite blasé about it all.

Why was there such animosity, bordering on hatred, towards my mother? Here is a little bit of background knowledge I feel that helped to make her the person Nana had become.

She met my grandfather through a lonely-hearts column. After six years of courtship with another man, in fact she'd been engaged to him, she was jilted. He had been seeing another woman in the latter stages of the relationship with Nana and was two-timing her. Within six months, Nana's fiancé had married the other woman, leaving Nana high and dry.

In those days, should a person who was officially engaged to that person, do what Nana's betrothed did, constituted a 'breach of contract' and could be sued in a court of law. Nana, I believe, was a very bitter woman when she met up with my Grandad.

Both Nana and Grandad married on the rebound, *he* to get over the death of his wife, and *she* to get over the heinous fashion in which Nana had been treated, by being jilted. Theirs was a love-hate relationship, which somehow worked for them.

Nana was the only girl in her family, with three other siblings, Bill, Ted and Rose's husband, Charlie. He was, however, a very good darts player. He would make his own flights from goose feathers, I believe.

All three brothers went to war and were injured in some shape or form. Usually fingers missing or damaged. Bill, however, had one of his legs broken, when a piece of shrapnel from enemy fire had also torn away a large chunk of flesh. Amazingly, even with the injured leg resembling a Fyffes banana, he could walk as fast as anybody else.

How they met, I don't know, but Bill married a seamstress called 'Ada', who came from Holdernesse Road, near Tooting Beck Station in London. She was a very attractive woman and was 20 years younger than Bill – but they loved each other dearly. Ada would sew the costumes for the actors and actresses in the theatres, such as Drury Lane, the Hippodrome and others. She would do the alterations to make them fit properly.

Uncle Ted, as I called him, was married to Aunt Doll.

To protect me from the violence that used to go on at the Cosy Café, when schooldays were taking place it was arranged for me to have my meals at a neighbour's house, on the other side of the road. After finishing my schooling at Church Street School in All Saints Road, I would go straight to this other house until approximately 6 o'clock, then come back to the café. My grandfather warned me that this arrangement concerning my meals had to work out. If it didn't, I would have to go into a children's home.

However, my big mouth wrecked this arrangement. I ended up staying at the Cottage Homes in Cosham, just outside of Portsmouth, not far from Portsdown Hill.

It happened like this. One day, the main meal consisted of a stew. One of the ingredients was pearl barley. Mistakenly, I associated the pearl barley as akin to chicken feed, the corn that was fed to the birds that provided the eggs. I refused to eat my dinner, "I'm not eating *that*, it's chicken feed", I said. "Excuse me," my neighbour said, "what did you say?" Three times I was asked to eat, three times I refused.

She dragged me back to the Cosy Café across the road. Many years later, with hindsight, I realised that spending most of my schooldays across the road was in a way for my own protection. When the fights took place, at the age of six years old, I used to think "wow, if grown-ups do this when they've grown up, I'll have some of that".

Two weeks later, my grandfather (with me in tow) was walking along Lake Road. What was I doing? I was having a temper tantrum, that's what. In my left hand, I was carrying a bundle of Dandie comics, and Beanos, whilst keeping up a kicking tantrum at my Grandad's leg. He didn't say a word.

Eventually, we both arrived at the 'Cottage Homes'. I was shown where I would sleep in the dormitory – my grandfather then left.

My big mouth *still* used to get me into more trouble than enough, even in the Cottage Homes. Talking at mealtimes – verboten

– forbidden.  Many was the time that I would be made to stand outside the canteen in the foyer facing the corner, complete with a dunce's hat, with a large letter 'D' on it, to become a source of ridicule.  In short, I hated it there.  If only I had kept my big mouth shut at Lake Road, there, but for the Grace of God, go I.

Which reminds me, I cannot remember a time when I never went to Sunday School, even in the Cottage Homes (in the plural because there were two homes, one for the boys and one for the girls, and ne'er the twain shall meet).

I've mentioned my going to Sunday School for a reason. Although I was made to go, I never protested about it as I quite enjoyed the experience.

I can remember going to 'The Church of the Good Shepherd' in Lake.  Also going to a little chapel in Ventnor after my mother had absconded with me.  Going to school, at Church Street School, Sunday afternoons once again were used to promote the Gospel message

# Chapter 2

## *City life, for a while*

"It was the best of times, it was the worst of times" to quote a leading figure in a book written about the French Revolution.

Thus it was so during my formative years of growing up, from the age of seven until my entry into Newport County Secondary Grammar School at Nodehill, Newport, when Headmaster Stan Ward was in charge as the Headmaster.

I was taken away from the Cottage Homes and brought back to a new home in Cuthbert Road, Fratton. Cuthbert Road was one of the many roads leading from St. Mary's Road, which in turn tee'd into Fratton Road, which had St. Mary's Church at its junction.

As a youngster, this little terrace house at No.8 was in the perfect spot for a 'would-be' child aspiring to be an adult in a children's world.

There were times of despair, when my mother came there to visit her dad (my grandfather). Always, but always, a confrontation would take place involving Nana and my mother.

I was brought up to hate my mother, by Nana, because of her abandonment of me, when I was left in St. Mary's hospital in Newport at the time of my birth. By the way, during the turn of the century in the early 1900s, the place where I was housed was known as the workhouse! Humble beginnings indeed. I refer to St Mary's Hospital, Newport.

Sheer bewilderment at seeing two grown women having a catfight and literally rolling around on the floor with them scratching at one another's faces and the hair-tugging contest, just left me numb with incredulity.

Even with pressure from Nan, I could not hate my own mother, no way. However, I never had the closeness that Nan *should*, in my opinion when thinking back on the matter, have encouraged. In a way, I became a surrogate son to my Nan, a child she never had.

I've thought hard and long as to why she should have been this way, why she could have been so vindictive. So, here are a few thoughts for what they're worth on the matter.

First, the isolation she must have felt when after six years of courtship she was jilted.

Secondly, she had very Victorian values. With Nana there were no shades of 'grey' in her mental make-up. On *any* subject imaginable, the outcome was either black or white.

Thirdly, something compelled her to win every argument (usually of her own making). She was only 5 feet 2 inches tall, but in spite of her being short in stature she was a fighter by nature, both physically and mentally.

Fourthly, being the head cook in one of the large hospitals at Milton, not far from Copnor in Portsmouth, she was used to giving orders, of being in charge. In fact, any tally-man who came to our door had to watch his 'P's and 'Q's or he'd get a good tongue lashing from her.

Fifthly, she wasn't *all* bad, although the proverbial picture I've painted of her thus far must seem that way. When she was in a good mood, she could almost charm the birds from the trees. I've got to admit that.

Sixthly, she might have been a hard act to follow – but she *was* fair. If I was too cheeky, "nobody answers me back" she'd say. I deserved whatever punishment she metered out. I did love her, in spite of her failings, and most of all I admired her tenacity, her fighting spirit. If I'm brutally honest, *she*, more than *anybody* in this world, helped to mould me into the person I've become, for which I am eternally grateful.

The one last word on this character observation, Nana, singlehandedly, brought me up. You see, Grandad showed no interest whatsoever in my progress through life. How could he have? His wife, my maternal grandmother, died aged 42, although from the

Death Certificate she was 43, in the Summer of 1942. My ensuing birth, in all likelihood, could, and most probably did, help to bring about her demise.

If nothing else in life is important, I believe that my being able to see *both* sides of any coin is a gift that the Good Lord has given me, that can help one to be *true* to oneself – and *others*.

Well that's enough of blowing my own trumpet, let's get back to life at the sharp end at Cuthbert Road.

Life at the sharp end of Cuthbert Road wasn't just a bowl of cherries for my grandfather. You see, he was the sole breadwinner in our little family, and he worked jolly hard to bring home the readies that paid for the food on the table – plus the bills.

His job? A labourer on the many building sites around Portsmouth – an unenviable task. Let me explain. He was a hod carrier for the brickies. His job was to carry umpteen bricks in a carrier called a hod up and down ladders. When that part of his job was over with for the time being, he would be mixing cement. This entailed pushing a heavily loaded-up wheelbarrow along the labyrinth of planks, usually positioned at what I thought were steep angles, to the bricklayer who, in my mind, had, although a more *skilled* job, an *easier* one to boot.

In Wintertime, when the weather was cold, his callused hands showed real signs of wear. Coupled with the water, the cement and the coldness of winter, his hands or fingers would split open. It wasn't until he returned home, after a hard day's graft, that his hands would come around (thaw out). Whilst they were cold the pain wouldn't manifest itself. However, I've seen tears, literally, come to his eyes, with the intense pain with the 'chaps' on his fingers. He was in a hellava lot of pain, but he was stoic. He never complained. This is when Edie (Nana) rallied round her man, to care for him the best she could.

Grandfather *still* volunteered to work whatever overtime he could. Being a grafter, he usually got his wish.

Now to me – and what living in a major city had to offer.

First, my schooling at Penhale Road junior mixed school.

Second, close proximity to the recreation ground, off Goldsmith Avenue.

Third, believe it or not, going to the local Anglican Church, the Church of St Boniface.

Fourth, the cinema – the Odeon, also another cinema for the Saturday Morning Matinee.

Fifth, the bomb sites that littered the city. They were idyllic. A young boy's paradise.

My days at Penhale Road I would view with mixed feelings. Two teachers stand out from all the other teachers.

The first, Mr L, who I considered to be an utter and compete sadist. Those days, during the 1950s, were the days of corporal punishment, when we were caned if we misbehaved.

My big mouth got me into more trouble than enough, I've got to admit that.

"Bettenson!" he'd shout out. "Keep quiet!" But Bettenson didn't always button it, or keep quiet, did he?

"Ok. You, at the front, move it!"

"Who sir, me sir?"

"Yes sir, you sir, out the front and stand by my desk."

Then, the mental torture began. In the corner of the classroom was a cupboard. In that cupboard was a selection of canes – ten of them in all. He would then proceed to go through the ritual of doing a dummy run with each and every cane, until the decision to arm himself with the appropriate weapon.

"Hold your hand out straight boy, palms uppermost – don't move – or you'll get a double dose of the same medicine."

Some people learn things the hard way. I was certainly no exception to the rule. The very first time I had the cane, I vowed to myself that however painful, I would not cry. There were girls as well as boys in the classroom. It was so quiet I swear you could hear a pin drop.

As Mr L. made a few practise moves with the cane of his choice, I steeled myself for the inevitable. When it came to the ultimate and final word in the saga, I watched the cane's descent onto my outstretched hand. At the last touch of the cane on my hand, I flinched. It was involuntary, I couldn't help it. The cane caught me on the fingertips of my right hand. I'd messed up.

"I warned you boy, *not* to move, did I not?" he said.

"Now, hold your hand out again boy, and this time do as you are told."

The secret? To close one's eyes until the cane had landed. With mixed emotions, and tears *wanting* to well up but not materialising, I did get a little satisfaction from the admiring looks from the girls in the class, for what it's worth!

Now to my favourite teacher – Mr O'Neil.

Mr O'Neil took an interest in two people in my class at Penhale Road. I was one, the other was Fiona, from bonny Scotland. She was from the Lowlands and spoke with a beautiful soft Scottish accent. To hear her 'reading at sight' was a joy to behold. Both she and I shone in that class under the direction of our Form Teacher, Mr O'Neil, and he encouraged us a lot, impressing upon us the need to study and learn as much as we could, due to the onset of an exam called the 11 Plus.

He even gave us homework although it was extra curriculum. We both didn't have to do it, but it made sense so to do.

Under his guidance, we excelled in class, and in fact, come the day of the exam, we romped through it – and passed.

I was offered a scholarship at the Southern Grammar School, Portsmouth. It was this offer that made up my Guardians' minds to return to the Island once more, where I was offered a place at Newport County Secondary Grammar School, in Nodehill. A wonderful opportunity to increase one's knowledge and to learn Languages (Latin, French, German) etc.

I am eternally grateful to the Good Lord, for giving me many talents. In my heart of hearts, I knew that I'd never be 'championship' material, but when giving my best, I could certainly offer a decent challenge. In most sports I'd shown an interest in, I both enjoyed and competed well.

My best friend in school was a lad called Michael Edgelar. He and I were picked many times to represent our school at Alexander Park. I was exceptional in the high jump discipline, before the days of the so-called 'Fosbury Flop'. For me, it was the western roll; also sprinting, the '100 yards dash' as we called it.

Plays were acted out in Wesley Central Hall, and a long walk would take us to St Mary's Church. This churchyard, by the way, had a wonderful mature, horse-chestnut tree. During the conker season, we kids would throw huge pieces of wood at the tree, to obtain the best of the 'conker-material'. Happy days.

Just to illustrate the mentality of the kids growing up in a bomb-damaged city, one day I was kicked in the groin area, by a girl in the same year as myself. I dropped like a stone. She ran away laughing. To her, it was one big joke. I failed to see the funny side – I didn't even know her name. C'est la vie, n'est pas?

Secondly, close proximity to the recreation ground gave me many happy days. My first job that I had, on coming home from school, was to walk the dog, that was called 'Nigger' (after a colour called Nigger Brown). In those halcyon days of the early 50s, there was very little racism.

A firm called 'Robertson's' had a slogan, 'Look for the Golly', the golly on the jar. Each jar of jam or marmalade sported a picture of a black golliwog. If enough paper 'golliwogs' were saved up, they could be traded in for an 'enamel' brooch. Also, the Black & White Minstrel Shows were very popular, where *white* men would 'blacken-up' their faces. Al Jolson would sing 'Climb Up On my Knee Sonny-Boy'.

In November, the firework season kicked off. We boys would go to a very quiet part of the park. We'd dig out small tunnels in the dirt, take the contents out of three or four penny bangers and light the blue touch paper. It was quite spectacular really. We would 'leg it' if the Park Attendant turned up, however.

We could play football with gay abandonment. I was a witness to a technical k.o. when a matelot got flattened as a football caught him a solid blow on the side of the head. He was sparko for several minutes.

Going to Sunday School, at the Church of St Boniface, a local Anglican church. If the truth be known, I really did enjoy going to Sunday School, usually during the afternoon on a Sunday, at 3pm.

Having gone to church at a very early age from cradle to the present time, aged seven to eight years old, I was getting a jolly good grounding in the things and ways of the Lord. It wasn't until I eventually got married, settled down and got saved at the age of 23, that I understood the grace of Salvation. This was to be a huge turning point in my Life, but more of that later.

Going to the theatres and cinemas such as the Gaumont, Odeon, Roxy etc, were all much of a muchness, in my opinion.

We kids would go to the Saturday morning matinees, which was quite enjoyable. However, I can clearly remember going to see QUO VADIS, when children could only enter if their parents were with them. We would go to the long lines of grown-ups and badger one of the grown-ups to take us kids in. We would split up, as we would have to go in singly, if the person of our choice agreed to allow us to accompany them. We'd hand over our money to each willing 'parent', and then, once inside, we would regroup, so as to be able to sit together and watch the film.

Was it wrong of us to do it? You bet your sweet life it was. We did however meet the recommendations of the cinema. We each came in, accompanied by an adult. The rules had not been broken, but they were severely bent.

Forbidden fruits? Sometimes they're the best, are they not?

In the late 1930s, early 1940s, Grandad used to be a drummer in a small dance band. He used to wear those shiny, patent shoes that ballroom dancers wear.

My mother Amy was an aspiring young thespian in a local amateur dramatic society. Her forte, however, was in her music. I have a photograph of her, at the age of 16, playing a full-sized piano key accordion. She could read music, but in the absence of a music sheet or score, she was stuffed.

She was unable to play a note by ear. With me, it's different. Everything I play, when getting to grips with my guitar, is by ear. I'm self-taught, you see.

With the Good Lord's help, I've both written and sung some of the Gospel songs that me and members of my family have sung in many of the smaller churches on this Island of ours.

Ryde Elim, The Church on the Roundabout, with Peter Rowe, Fort St. Sandown's Assemblies of God, Blackgang Christian Mission, Cowes Congregational, the Congregational Church during a P.S.A. (Pleasant Sunday Afternoon) and last but not least, the Wayfarers, just off Carisbrooke High Street. Oh yes, I mustn't leave out Zion Chapel, in Ryde, Brian and Brenda Sexton's church.

Today, at the time of writing, it's now 6 a.m. in the morning, outside here on the outskirts of Ryde, it's once again a bright, sun-shiny day.

The only sounds are the cooing of the wood pigeons, the cheeping of the sparrow, an occasional fox's high-pitched yapping or just the sound of silence.

Years ago, an old feller by the name of Jack Hargreaves would come onto the goggle box – and talk on country ways. I'm reminded of the words of the signature tune when I look out of my eastward facing windows; the words are as follows:

*Trees everywhere, with blossoms in their hair, and mother nature wears her newest gown, oh what fun it is to be just out of town. With white fluffy clouds in a cluster, hanging on the breeze to dry (finishing with the sun polishing the blue, blue sky)*

When I look out on all of this, the world, my world here on the Island, seems at peace with itself. The air at 6 a.m. in the morning is clean, with little or no pollutants from motor borne traffic to spoil it, what bliss.

Earlier on, I mentioned the theatres. There were two we sometimes visited, the Theatre Royal and the Coliseum. There is nothing quite like the atmosphere of going to a live performance at a theatre, especially during the pantomime season, when the audience as one would belt out the words of Rule Britannia and sing along with the actors and actresses on stage.

Old time musicals where women would wear their large fancy hats. They would look the part when they'd put on their best bib and tucker, the men that is.

We would go to these homes of music hall, to let down our hair, relax, laugh, join in the antics on stage – and enjoy!

Before I continue any further, just a few words about my Grandad's war experiences. You see, during the First World War, i.e. WW1, many young men joined up because of the slogan 'Your Country Needs You'. My grandad was no exception.

He was born Frederick William Chambers, one of the four sons of Maurice Chambers, who ran a small dairy farm in Adgestone, not far from Sandown. (Frederick, Maurice, Herbie and Arthur).

I met up with a Mrs Munns, I think her name was. She was a guide at Morton Manor near Brading, a woman well into her nineties. Her mind was as sharp as a razor, with no outward show of frailty. A remarkable woman. I asked her, due to her longevity, if she remembered the four Chambers brothers. She certainly did – I was thrilled to bits by this and thanked her profusely, what a lady.

But I digress. Fred was born in 1899, and he enlisted in a Hampshire Regiment in 1914 I believe, at the age of 15 years. He did his training, especially with horses, learning, he said, to ride from a slow walk, a trot, a canter, a gallop and finally to a stretch gallop.

His job? To drive a team of four horses towing a limber or gun carriage, the field guns that were used in that era. He would be riding the left-hand lead horse with his right leg encased in a protective leg-guard. This leg-guard was to protect it from being crushed by the bodies of the two lead horses, when on occasions there would be a 'coming together' of the horses' bodies, especially when travelling at speed and turning to left or right.

For his trouble, I don't know the date, but when he was in the Gallipoli campaign, in the Dardenelles, he was buried alive. A bomb landed just yards from one of the trenches the soldiers were sheltering in. Mud, slime, and filth from the heavy rains etc meant his mates digging him out of that hellhole. After he was buried alive under tons of earth, he was brought back to Blighty – his nerves shot to pieces, strapped to a hospital bed for his own protection. He had what was called the 'Delirium Tremors' the so-called D.Ts.

The nursing staff honestly did not know if he'd eventually recover or end up a raving lunatic. Cannon fodder, that's all our young men, the flower of British manhood, had become. A war of attrition. I'll also add, it was thus so for the Germans. I'm talking about the common or garden soldiers *on both* sides now.

In 1973 – 1975, I worked in Germany as an aircraft fitter, alongside an older German called Kasper Kränzle. He was an engineer in the Panzer division, wounded, becoming an American Prisoner of War. I worked in a Messerschmidt Bilcov Blöm (M.B.B.) factory, as an aircraft sheetie (sheet metal worker). Sometimes, we were put on other jobs, the one with Kasper was the 'Sandstralle' or shot blasting booth. One would have to insert one's hands into two huge great gauntlet gloves pre-attached to the machine. I enjoyed it –

especially the company of Kasper Kränzle. He even invited me to stay with him on some weekends.

On a Saturday morning's overtime, each alternative Saturday, we'd take turns cooking an English breakfast or a German breakfast. We forged a strong bond of friendship, in spite of us being on opposite sides during the war.

In fact, when my time at M.B.B. was done, the contract our company had was ramping down, instead of up. Kasper was in tears. We both enjoyed each other's company. Parting however was sweet sorrow. He was a 'diamond geezer' albeit a Deutsch one.

Back to my grandfather. He did recover – else I would not be here would I? He eventually settled down, worked in the Merchant Navy, met an Irish girl called Kathleen (Kitty) and had one child, Amy Kathleen. The rest is history.

Although Nan and Grandad had become bankrupt, with just enough money to buy number 8 Cuthbert Road, they organised the Coronation street party. I've still got the be-ribboned invitation with the red, white and blue colours on it.

This, obviously, was one of the many 1953 Coronation street parties. We had a Coronation committee, with Fred and Edie in charge, with most of the other committee members made up from the neighbours living close by.

It *was* a great success. The food was excellent. The party games were carried out in the local recreation ground. There was music. It was good to be alive on such an occasion.

To grow up in a big city, one becomes very street-wise. This next illustration is the only account I'll give concerning the niceties of street fighting.

Picture two boys, one a ten year old, the other, a slightly built nine year old. The two boys, after an argument, decide to fight. The bigger one of the two boys indicates to the younger one his intention to take off his jacket. Whilst both arms are temporarily occupied, the smaller lad sees his chance, leaps forward, kicks the bigger lad in the groin and on the way down he punches his opponent in the head - night, night, nurse. The smaller lad has won. Not quite in keeping with the Queensbury Rules! In Portsmouth, in the back streets literally it could be 'kill or be killed' as the saying goes.

Why did I feel the need to mention this? At the age of eighteen, Michael Edgeler, my best mate at Penhale Road Junior mixed school, was knifed to death outside Pompey Dockyard. His crime? He would not join the so-called Apprentices dock-yard strike in support of the dockies who were already out on strike.

Michael lived somewhere in or near Arundel Street. Michael Rencourt, another school chum and a third lad panicked. If they snitched to the authorities, what then – will the same happen to them if they grassed up on their apprentice mates? They half-dragged their stricken mate, half carried him home to Arundel Street, a mile away. Mike lost so much blood, he literally bled to death. They got him home, but at what cost? This is what it can be like, growing up in a big city. I know, because I was once part of that life.

Soon, I was to return back to my roots, back home to the Island I love, after I passed the 11+ exam.

I was offered a place at Portsmouth Southern Grammar school, but went instead to Newport County Secondary Grammar, Nodehill.

# Chapter 3

## *The Home-Coming*

My grandfather applied for, and got, a gardening job at a huge mansion and country estate called Oaklawn, at Wootton. This mansion was on the way to what is called the Foreshore, at the mouth of Wootton Creek. Originally it was bought by an Admiral Hutton and his wife.

When the Admiral died, his widow employed a lady companion to care for her. We were picked up by, what seemed to me, to be a huge black limousine. I'll never forget the number-plate, of DL 8969 – don't ask me why, I don't know.

The next two and a half years were to be the happiest years of my young life. Our dwelling was the Lodge at Oaklawn which was at the entrance. To the back of the Lodge were the stables which could easily house the coaches, drawn by the horses that were obviously stabled there.

I would walk to Wootton Bridge, a mile away, in wet weather or fine. I was pretty fit in those days, and during my second year (or was it the third?) I would turn out for the school football team. One year, our school shared the honours with Sandown Grammar School in the Baring Shield. We drew in the final at Sandown.

Why the home-coming? What makes the time spent at Oaklawn so very special? The neighbours in this neck of the woods were completely different to the working class life-style I'd just left behind in Portsmouth. To the left of Oaklawn was a beautiful dwelling owned by Colonel Minshall. Down the road, still on the same side of the road, lived Colonel Mew and his family.

Across the road was Lisle Court, complete with tennis court. It was owned by Colonel de-Lang-Long. Mister and Mrs Westmacott were the butler and chambermaid.

They all seemed to speak with cut-glass accents, were very articulate in what they had to say, and were always polite.

Why should my two and half year stay at Oaklawn, Wootton be such a big deal for me?

First, the absolute freedom of the place. It was deep in the countryside. Secondly, the sheer vastness (it seemed) of its size, with the private beach just to the right of Woodside Bay. Thirdly, the fishing. There were very old, large prawning nets at the old house.

There's an old saying: 'Manners maketh man' and I learned the added advantages of being polite, not getting above one's station, (full of oneself) and being, above all, honest. Honesty being the best policy.

It was idyllic. Living here was a far cry from being in the back streets of a major city. A far cry from hitching a lift along the road, on the tailboard of a lorry. Of going to Baffins Pond, roaming to Langstone Harbour. A far cry indeed from frequenting one of the bomb sites littered across Portsmouth. We boys (no girls allowed, that was 'cissy' as we called it) would just use the brickbats that were all over the bombsites to hurl at whatever bottles we could find.

On occasions, we'd come across a pole, pointed at one end, which would have been used to 'site-up' the ground prior to building on it. This pole, although heavy, doubled as a spear or javelin. On occasions we'd have to scarper, as this did not go down too well with the building or site engineers. General rough and tumbling, wrestling with each other, just as boys being boys, it was all part of growing up.

However, once more I digress. Take my third point, which was fishing. At the mouth of Wootton Creek, at very low tide, are some rocks just to the east of Woodside Bay. Around these rocks was an abundance of prawns, which swam around the seaweed encrusted rocks. I never, ever, went back empty-handed. Although I very nearly copped it, when I was cut off by the tide. Making my way back to dry land, I was literally up to my neck in the waters of the incoming tide.

Dangerous? You bet your sweet life it was dangerous – I couldn't swim!

Fourthly, my last point – the very countryside itself. Smells of the pines that grew in abundance, the fragrance of the flowers, the roses, lavender and many other plants. The very smell of nature itself permeated the air. Early in the morning, the red squirrels would be in abundance. The high-pitched yap of the fox, especially at dusk, staccato-like in its bark, would sound so very sharp in its intensity especially during the mating season.

I could go on and on about the birds that frequented the orchard and would try to invade the fruit trees that were cordoned off from the rest of the large garden by nets, strung over the trees by poles, to keep out the birds.

You see, one bird on a fruit tree, whether it be apple, pear, plum, raspberry etc, could wreak absolute havoc. One bird, often a jay, would peck a hole in every single item of fruit, ruining the entire crop, if allowed to do so.

To my mind, the jay was, is, one of the most beautiful looking birds among the birds found in the British Isles. Its vivid colouration, especially the pale blue on its plumage, was a wonderful sight. What was my grandfather's solution to this intruder, this destroyer of his hard-earned labours as a gardener?

He would hang the poor bird out on some string attached to a bamboo pole, after dashing the poor bird's brains out (I suspect partly in retribution for ruining his fruit crop). Bear in mind my grandfather came from a farming community. There's no sentimentality when one's livelihood is threatened, especially by a bird. Did the festooning of a dead bird hanging from a bamboo pole make any difference? I don't think so, after all, our flying friends are bird-brained, aren't they? Think about it.

The grounds of Oaklawn must have been about three to four acres, easily, in size. As one drives through the main gates, to the right of the long drive to the main house, is the Paddock. The Paddock, for obvious reasons, could be used for the horses. In fact, this one-acre field called the Paddock was full of abundance of hay in one of the years we were living at Oaklawn. Although we were never very 'close', as the saying goes, because of his farming background, grandad taught me most of the skills of the countryside.

Side by side, but offset by a couple of metres, we scythed through the standing hay. It took us two whole days – it was hard work, thirsty work. As soon as the dew was off the grass, we cut the hay until late evening. It took us two ten-hour days, we barely stopped for lunch. It was ideal for cutting as it was similar to standing corn, in that it hadn't been flattened by the wind. It's therefore easier, and quicker, to cut when in this state.

We made a proper hayrick a few days later when it was deemed dry enough to harvest. A local farmer bought it off the old lady, the lady companion to Admiral Hutton's wife.

Another skill I learned was the art of using a two-handed cross-cut saw. Also, being able to wield a cross-axe, enabled me to make my presence felt in some small way.

Coming back to the Island was to facilitate my Grammar School education. In fact, my grandfather had to go cap in hand to speak with Stan Ward, the headmaster of Newport County Secondary Grammar School.

There was what I call a 'slush fund', whereby people with no real means to fund the expensive uniform and the P.E. kit (which comprised football stockings, boots, leg shields and a host of other sundries, for example a leather school satchel) were all catered for by the Headmaster, Stan Ward, for which I am eternally grateful.

The teaching staff were tremendous. 'Mac' Mackinley was our PE teacher. He had an English accent but was Scottish to the core. When doing our physical exercises in the school playground, he would accompany the exercises by *whistling*, yes whistling, one of the many Scottish Airs.

The first thing we had to do was to run up the length of Mount Pleasant Road, head off towards Watergate Road, bear left at the roundabout-come-crossroads and return back to school via College Road, running up to the top of Mount Pleasant Road via a different direction. The main reason we hurried back? To play football, albeit with a tennis ball. Happy days.

Mr Reay (disrespectfully referred to as 'cry-baby' Johnny Ray, after the pop singer) was a brilliant teacher regarding our woodworking classes. Simply the best.

Mrs Corben is next. I did not understand many of the aspects of mathematics. However, in layman's language, in a language I could understand, she would simplify various factors that formed the basis of maths, long division and multiplication of large numbers, the hard way without calculators. Geometry, theorems, circles, triangles, all the various aspects of what a mathematician needs to work out the correct answers, gleaned from given facts. I grew to love maths.

Miss Tottle, the close-cropped short-haired disciplinarian, or so she seemed to be in year one and two, taught English. I grew to love studying both English Literature and English Grammar, which incidentally, in some small way, is why I can (I hope) put pen to paper in an interesting way.

Hence of course, the writing of this, my first book.

Returning now to countryside pursuits. Literally, the pursuit of foxes, or fox hunting. Hopefully, what I am about to write concerning this 'sport', for want of a better word, may clarify the pros and con on the subject.

Next door to Oaklawn lived Colonel Minshall and his wife. When the Master of Hounds and the Whipper-in (the man who managed the hounds) came next door, it was as a guest of the Minshalls, who would bring out a celebratory drink (the stirrup cup) before the hunt would commence.

The Master of the Hounds, and the Whipper-in, were both in their hunting pink - goodness knows why 'pink' when their uniforms were bright red - I'll never know.

One Saturday, the hounds caught and killed the vixen, a female fox that had been an absolute nightmare to one of the Wootton farmers. On Sunday, the very next day, the gamekeeper shot the male dog-fox.

"John, go and get an axe and a block of wood from the shed. We're going to that field opposite Woodside Bay Naturist (nudist colony) centre." When I got to the field, I beheld the most beautiful creature that nature allows us to share our lives with on planet Earth.

This fox was in its prime. He had a magnificent gingery coloured coat. He was a handsome specimen of an animal, cut short in its prime, for the temerity to go hunting on the farmer's land for chickens.

I never went fox-hunting again, which I used to enjoy. And the 'trophy'? The 'reward' for being given the opportunity to take home a 'souvenir'? The fox's tail (or brush). As far as I know, it's still hanging up on the nail where I left it.

In mitigation however, not many people realise the *good*, yes good, that the Isle of Wight Hunt do, out there in the community. They pick up dead animals and help dispose of them, amongst many other things. Fox-hunting has now been banned although the 'fox' has now been substituted by a trail-blazer who seeks to be the quarry of being hunted.

Fox-hunting has been entrenched in British farming life. It's part of our culture. That's all I have to say on the matter. My time is now over concerning Oaklawn, as we move on to Newport.

# Chapter 4

*Beginning Working Life*

Grandfather felt the need to be closer to Newport and got a job as the curator of two cemeteries.

I was thirteen and a half years old when we made the move from Wootton to Newport. One cemetery, the oldest building, was nearer Newport town centre. It was situated in Fairlee Road. The other house, the best one of the two houses, was situated in Halberry Lane. Nana and Grandad should have moved into the newest of the two houses allocated to the Curator, and to the Assistant Curator, but opted instead for the Fairlee Road house which was closer to the shopping centre.

The cemetery at Fairlee Road was established in 1858 but the cemetery at Halberry Lane was not established until 1899. In fact, St Paul's Church Barton boasted a church and graveyard but because only six years of its life was remaining for any future deaths/burials, the cemetery at the other end of Halberry Lane was designated to be an extension (to become an 'overflow' cemetery) due to its sister cemetery being nearly full up.

If my memory serves me right, there used to be four men to work in the two cemeteries, the Curator, Assistant Curator and two others. Grandfather's duties as Curator was to book in the dates and times available to ensure enough time was allocated for the digging of the graves. He had to ensure the correct plot of land was designated to the correct place on the chart, for official purposes.

I can remember on one occasion, two middle-aged women coming to pay their respects at the same grave – even though their two loved ones were both buried in the cemetery, obviously one of the ladies was wrong in her calculation as to where her beloved was buried. A tribunal or court had convened, ultimately culminating in the grave being exhumed. The tell-tale brass burial plate on the now rotted coffin lid eventually became the deciding factor as to who *was* actually buried there. One of the aforesaid ladies was in tears, the other lady – absolutely elated.

My grandfather did *not* have to do grave-digging duties; he could delegate that responsibility to one of the younger men. However, he was too obstinate and stubborn for his own good. He *was* 57 years old for goodness sake, but he wanted the overtime money regardless of his lumbago. Chè sera, sera.

Sometimes, around Christmas time, there would be a few fun and games when the variegated holly would start disappearing from the centre-circle not far from the entrance to Newport Cemetery. One night the police were lying in wait for the thieves – but nobody showed up. My grandfather, and the police for that matter, *knew* who the perpetrators were but had to catch them red-handed. No chance of that happening. The holly wreaths the holly was intended for would have to wait a while.

Let's get back to my education again. I learned three languages at school, Latin – which I hated – French, and German. French was taught by Miss Wadley. She had a wind-up, old fashioned gramophone. Miss Wadley was very well spoken and we must assume her diction concerning her French would have been perfect also. She was a rather temperamental sort of individual and we students would sometimes try to wind her up. On occasions we would succeed and Miss Wadley would be almost in tears. She soldiered on however to live and last out another day, naughty though we were.

Mr David Marr taught German, which I loved. I learned it for three years at school. During my contract work in Germany for close on two years from 1973 – 1975, the three years of 'Schule-Deutsch' or school-German, did me in good stead as I honed my theory concerning the German grammar with the practical by actually speaking it to German factory workers and knowing enough to get by when going to the shops. Wunderbar, jah?

Believe it or not, Morning Assembly, which always started one's day, I looked forward to. We would start with a hymn and a pupil, usually a 6th Former, would read a passage of scriptures then would come the announcements. A would-be aspiring pianist would play classical music on the grand piano as we filed out of the assembly hall.

In my five years of grammar school training, I can only recall one public (yes public) caning, of a boy who was deemed to have brought shame and disgrace on the school, bringing it into disrepute. To howls of delight, he was kicking and booting his school cap down the street by Shutlers shop, in Nodehill.

After bending over on stage during the morning assembly, he was given three strokes of the cane – and suspended from school for two weeks. That was the only time I can honestly say that I witnessed corporal punishment in full view of a captive audience.

Now and again my big mouth would land me in detention – for talking in class. On one such occasion, the hour-long session was overseen by Miss Wadley, the previously mentioned French teacher. Now Miss Wadley was very intelligent but (in my opinion) somewhat highly strung. There were ten of us in detention on the evening in question, and unfortunately a working party was repairing some of the loose tarmac on the pavement. One of the workmen started up on what was the final operation to flatten the new tarmac down with what I would term a 'thumping machine'. Because of the rhythmic thump, thump, thump of this machine, one wag in the detention room struck up the Anvil Chorus.

Very quickly, the whole class of detainees doing their penance were in fine voice. Miss Wadley was clearly out of her depth! With some teachers, one would not dare to cross the line as we did, but Miss Wadley had lost control and with a cry of anguish told us all to get out!

She'd had enough, and we? Well, we enjoyed a half an hour off of our 60 minute detention – what a result! People power had won (or should I say pupil power) and had triumphed for once.

If I'm honest, my grammar school prowess (for want of a better word) would be a respectable Mr Average. In a class of 28 say, I would be somewhere in the centre-ish.

I was now coming up to my 16th birthday in January. The following year I was due to take approximately eight, possibly nine, 'O' Level exams. Then, in December of my fifteenth year, our class had a visitor from the John Samuel White's shipyard. His name was Vic Newbury.

He gave a talk about the shipyard itself, and, after *very little* thought, I agreed to begin a five year apprentice-ship at J.S.White's.

I began my time as a prospective Fitter/Turner just after Christmas, a few days *before* my 16th birthday. At last, I could begin to repay Nana and Grandad, as I'd now begun a career that would change my life completely. My first week's pay? £2 and a halfpenny. Two Pounds and One Halfpence – a princely sum indeed!

My first week's pay soon shot up to £2-10 shillings and a halfpenny. £2-10s-½p. Whoopy-do! I was now in the money, I was now 16 years old and thought I knew it all. I had a lot to learn – in more ways than one.

To supplement this meagre wage, when other lads I'd grown up alongside had got 'ordinary' jobs, I would go mushrooming. This, obviously, was only in late August/September time when the heavy dew on the ground would draw them and their growth would be established very quickly.

I would get up at first light and walk along the path running from Seaclose recreation ground, parallel to the river Medina. It would take me about 20 minutes to walk there and I got to know which farmers' fields yielded the best crop. Usually, they were the 'white-cap' mushers, but occasionally I'd stumble upon a 'horse-mushroom' which were much, much larger and were darker in colour – and could fetch a good price in the greengrocer's shop that I sold my mushrooms to. Now and again I'd take some to work and sell them – albeit more cheaply than my workmates would pay in the shops. C'est la vie, that's life.

On my first day alongside other would-be Fitter/Turners, we young lads were warned of the bad language that was rife in the shipyard. The chargehand who gave us the pep talk? Charlie Bettenson or 'Betto' as he was often referred to. He needn't have bothered, because I had honed my skills concerning the niceties of the Queen's English in the backstreets of Portsmouth. In all probability, I could teach my superiors a few extra ones thrown in of my own, tho' nowadays I would be loath to admit it.

Arthur Kilmartin, another chargehand, seemed to take me under his wing. He was a tall, unassuming, middle-aged man, quiet-mannered, but a person not to be taken for granted. If I did as I was told and did my job to the best of my ability, he was a good encourager and he was fair. I liked him a lot.

There were two jobs we apprentices, especially the first-year ones, did. Pipe-jamming and polishing up the hand-wheels which would go on the valve chests until they shone. Take pipe-jamming – there were literally hundreds of them, different pipes obviously, of every shape and size.

What on earth is pipe-jamming, you may ask? Pipe-jamming entails 'facing' the flanges of each pipe by the use of files. A course or 'bastard' file would be the order of the day, followed by a 'second-cut' file, then a medium-course file, ending up with a fine-file. A large square face-plate, smothered with blue marking dye, was necessary to place onto the flange of the pipe which would be gripped securely in a large vice.

This blue dye on the face-plate would provide the 'witness-mark' on the flange. We were expected to achieve an 85% coverage of the marking dye on the flange before facing the next pipe.

The next stage of the game was to water test each system of pipes - saturated and superheated steam pipes, diesel generator system, the circulating system. The pipes for the de-salinometers (a system where sea-water could be 'desalinated' having the salt from the seawater extracted) were steel pipes. Copper shop produced many copper pipes too and the sound of the planishing hammers, as the 'wrinkles' on the inside curve of the pipes had to be 'dressed' or smoothed out.

Before I carry on with the rest of my journey through life, J.S.White's shipyard, how did it come about?

It started its operation in 1802. The White family, from Broadstairs, Kent, had a long history of ship building beginning with the construction of the Royal Navel Cutter which was called 'Lapwing' in 1763 – 1764.

Colonel John White was born in 1665 in Caroline, Virginia, USA. He died on the 23$^{rd}$ March 1729 aged 64 years.

John Samuel White was a member of the Broadstairs family of White's (1838 – 1915). This John White was the founder of what would become the largest shipyard in Cowes. The firm came to prominence during the 20$^{th}$ Century and they became famous for building destroyers.

I first worked on a Blackwood class frigate, called the Kuthar. This was one of the three vessels built for the Indian Navy. Altogether, 12 frigates were built for the Royal Navy. They were being built as second rate, anti-submarine frigates until the late 1970s.

HMNZS Taranaki was an anti-submarine frigate built for the RNZN escort force throughout the 1960s and 1970s. HMS Arethusa, that I worked on in 1963, was a Leander-class frigate, launched in 1963 and commissioned by the Royal Navy on 24$^{th}$ November 1965.

She was used as a target for the Royal Navy – and sunk in June 1991. She was the last warship to be built at the Cowes shipyard.

The cross-Channel vessels Caesarea and Sarnia for the Channel Islands operated side by side and were in service from 1960 to the late 1970s. Their demise came with the introduction of the car ferry.

Apart from the larger vessels that I've mentioned, smaller vessels too were built by J.S.White's, for example the lifeboats. I once worked on a small coaster called the Celtic. She was captained by a Mr Sheath. When the vessel came in, she was making an awful racket. Apparently, Captain Sheath had ordered a new 'prop' shaft.

The original propeller shaft was lying at the bottom of the hold. Anyway, Sheathy said to 'Betto', "I don't understand it. I've only just splashed out for a new propshaft, and the racket when she picks up speed to say 7 or 8 knots is a killer."

Anyway, we dutifully changed the new propeller for another new propeller – and the same thing happened. Intense noise and vibration.

Sheathy, by this time, was nearly in tears. He'd paid out for two new prop shafts and neither of them was any good. Betto then had a brainwave. Pointing down to the bottom of the ship's hold, he said, "Is that the original shaft?"

Sheathy replies, "Yes, what difference will it make?"

Betto says, "I want the length of it measured against the length of the new prop shafts".

The *new* prop shaft, that was made by another firm, was two inches *longer*.

"That's what's wrong." says Betto. "If we cut 2in off the new shaft, that should do the trick."

You see, there was too much overhang by the propeller itself aft of the 'A' bracket.

"Well, I'm not paying for the other prop shaft." says Sheathy.

"Oh yes you are!" says Betto.

"We here at J.S. White's sussed out what was wrong, didn't we? Your other firm made a shaft causing more problems didn't they? Your beef is with them for messing you up, not with *us*."

And so it turned out. Betto was a good chargehand, he had a good headpiece on him.

Now what was the difference between the East Cowes Yard from that of the West Cowes one? Answer, *all* the difference in the world.

However, once again, I feel the need to digress. You see, whilst living in Portsmouth something profound happened. Should I have been born as a stick of rock, one would see the words 'Pompey Football Club' printed right the way through me, should anyone risk taking a bit, metaphorically speaking of course.

Two incidents spring to mind. The first is about football and how Pompey dealt with a certain 'wizard of the dribble' Stanley Matthews. Well, to put it bluntly, during the first five minutes of play, should poor old Stan so much as get a sniff of the ball, a crunching tackle would ensue.

Jimmy Scoular (Scottish), a formidable tackler, Duggie Reid, Norman Uprichard (Northern Ireland), Reg Flewin, Phil Gunter, Jackie Henderson. All of these players would go in hard (and I do mean hard) in tackling poor Stan. I can guarantee Stan would become just one of the walking wounded, out on the wing. He'd have to limp his way through the next 85 minutes of play as a passenger on the wing.

By disabling arguably one of the best English players of this era (I didn't agree with these tactics by the way) Pompey reduced the opposition (Matthews played for Blackpool during this period of his career) down to 10 men.

In short, poor old Stan was as much use to Blackpool as a chocolate fireguard. The heated exchanges, the tackles coming fast and furious, did not abate until he was 'crocked'. Not a pretty sight to arguably one of the best English players to have played for England.

All's fair in love and war as they say, and whenever Blackpool came to Portsmouth to play their future away games, where was Stan? You've guessed it, he was at home, being 'rested'. Blackpool wouldn't risk their star player on the field of play at Pompey – they knew what would happen to him.

The second incident concerns a young lady who became my girlfriend. I'll not even mention her by her Christian name, such is the distain I feel towards her.

You see, she was a 'Saints' supporter, unbeknown to me when I met her. We went out together before the footballing season got underway, before I'd found out she supported Southampton F.C, Pompey's south coast rivals. This leaves a nasty taste in the mouth when I think about it.

Guess what? She went and did the dirty on me by going out with another Southampton supporter behind my back. I was well rid of her I can tell you. But what else can one expect from a scummer!

Now I've got that off my chest, let's get back to J.S. White's and the difference between the East and West Cowes shipyards, on each side of the River Medina.

# Chapter 5

## *Working at J.S. White's*

The differences between East and West of the two halves of J.S.White's complemented each other. You see, before the sites of J.S.White's were established, more than a mention should be made concerning a certain Joseph Nye, formerly known as Joseph Noy or Ney.

Be that as it may, Joseph Noy was an unknown shipbuilder, probably born in Hampshire, England. By serving his apprenticeship in the Royal Dockyard at Portsmouth, being discharged as a skilled shipbuilder in 1692, he eventually signed a contract with the Navy Board to build a warship called the 'Poole' at his shipyard in East Cowes. By the way, it was the 'East Cowes site' that was fitted out with the slipways which would launch many, many ships for the Admiralty.

The 'Navy Board' was the body responsible for the building of her fighting ships in the Royal Navy. The site formerly known locally in East Cowes as 'Nye's yard' was the forerunner to 'Falcon Yard' at East Cowes, I would imagine. Anyway Joseph Nye (born Joseph Noy and indeed buried as Joseph Noy) is or was the same man, commissioned by the Royal Navy to build a fifth-rate ship – the 'Poole'.

After the completion of the 'Poole' at East Cowes in 1696, the Navy Board offered Noy a contract to build another ship, in Jersey, this time a fourth-rate ship.

The term 'fourth-rate' was a ship of the line with 46 – 60 guns mounted. A 'fifth-rate' ship was the second smallest of the British Royal Navy used to categorise sailing warships. She would only have carried 40 guns, possibly 44 guns.

The 'rates', or categories, originated in the reign of Charles I and categories, according to the number of guns a vessel could carry, were used between the 17th and the 19th centuries.

Remember these were sailing vessels, perhaps the most famous ship-of-the-line being HMS Victory, mothballed at Portsmouth Dockyard with the 'iron clad' Warrior, parked outside the harbour wall.

At the onset of steam, the modern ships of the line, of which J.S. White's built a goodly number, effectively ended the 'rating system' which relied upon the number of guns to designate which rate a ship should be placed in.

Joseph Noy built therefore, the first Admiralty warship for the Royal Navy, which obviously was a sailing vessel, but definitely on the piece of land that would later on in history become the historic J.S.White's shipyard.

Incidentally, Joseph Noy (Nye in English circles) eventually, because of his prowess of building fine warships, came to the attention of 'Peter the Great' of Russia.

In 1698, Joseph Noy had financial problems, leaving East Cowes for London, owing the shipwrights money. In London, Czar Peter the Great of Russia had arrived. He was recruiting for skilled labour in order to improve the woefully inadequate Russian Navy. Joseph Noy, together with another experienced shipbuilder, John Deane, joined Peter the Great in Russia to improve and build up the Russian Navy, with ships-of-the-line, English style.

Why an English shipbuilder over, say, the Dutch shipbuilders? Easy to answer – English methods of construction relied on scientific principles of mathematics, whereas the Dutch, although fine shipbuilders, relied on traditional techniques and 'rule of thumb' measurements. Relying on carefully drawn out plans, therefore, anybody using these plans could build using the precise measurements required to achieve the perfection (perceived by Peter the Great) to be the best in Naval shipbuilding.

Peter the Great, eventually with the help of Joseph Noy and John Deane, worked together until John Deane died during the harsh winter of 1699, on the Czar's warships. Richard Coyens, another Hampshire shipwright, joined Noy and together they helped transform the Russian Navy.

But this is enough of Nye, who arguably began his shipbuilding career on the Isle of Wight at a boatyard which was on the site of J.S. White's. I could go on, but Noy or Nye (the English way of spelling his name) was to become a very famous man indeed.

East Cowes, as I've mentioned, became a launch-pad for its naval vessels. After the 'Poole' the world was his oyster when John Samuel White established the largest of the shipyards on the Island. 'Jane's Book of Fighting Ships' features many of the Naval vessels built in Cowes.

It is now 9 a.m. in the morning, and I've been writing and studying the content of these pages since 6 a.m. so time for breakfast and a nice cup of tea for now.

All of this chapter and possibly some of the next one, will feature my apprenticeship at John Samuel White's, also my marriage to Marian. (She was and is a Bobby Dazzler).

Falcon Yard, East Cowes, during its era as kingpin for the launching of ships, especially Admiralty Vessels in the days of its ownership by John Samuel White, was very important.

As I wrote before, it was in 1694 that the yard was established. J.S.White came to prominence in the Victorian Era by specialising in the construction of destroyers for the Royal Navy and export customers. The Cowes shipyard according to 'Grace's Guide to British Industry', a registered charity (No. 1154342) in this web publication, contains 141,991 pages of information plus 227,461 images on early companies.

The Cowes (East and West Cowes) shipyard, once established, was to supply ships to the Admiralty for 200 years or more. Paul Hyland, in his book, "Wight, Biography of an Island', explains the origins of the shipyard in 1802. In 1805 the Company was first founded by John White. It was in 1864 that John White's son, John Samuel White, applied high speed engines to lifeboats. He collaborated with George Belliss of Birmingham to implement this.

With the work being conducted at the Falcon Yard in East Cowes, it finally took off as a shipyard, establishing a good reputation for building ships for the Admiralty in the 1880s.

## The Sultan of Zanzibar's Barge

This was a vessel built in White's shipyard in the 1870s. The writer for Grace's Guide had worked on engineering projects in the Port of Zanzibar in 1987 and happened across a barge, a *very ornate* barge, with plush velvet seats below a canopy. A plaque, affixed to the barge, showed it was built at White's Shipyard here on the Island. Apparently, the Sultan of Zanzibar, who was the Sultan from 1870 to 1888, was invited to a state visit to England in 1875.

It was largely to ensure a period of friendliness and pacification, after the British Naval Actions in subduing the slave trade along the coast of East Africa.

On arrival at London Docks by the Sultan of Zanzibar, Queen Victoria had laid on a special Barge which had been built at the East Cowes shipyard. The barge was commissioned to be built and was to be towed up the Thames to Windsor. The Sultan was so impressed by this very ornate barge, that Queen Victoria presented it to him as a gift.

Possibly, this barge is one of the oldest surviving examples of White's 19th century workmanship.

The slipways at East Cowes were very impressive. They had to be as the Leander class anti-submarine frigates (Londonderry and Taranaki) were 372ft long. They were launched stern-first, from East Cowes, with copious addition of drag-chains to slow her passage across to the other side of the river Medina. The vessel only had approximately 10ft to spare on reaching the other side of the river.

A frigate is smaller than a destroyer, but larger than a corvette. The Leander class was the most successful design of the frigate of its day – a very, very valuable asset to the Royal Navy!

There were three Leander-class Type 12 anti-submarine frigates built at J.S. White's. The Londonderry 1958, the Taranaki 1959 (both Rothesay Class Type 12) and the last frigate to be built in J.S. White's shipyard was Arethusa in 1965.

What is the difference between a frigate and a destroyer? Generally speaking, a frigate is a type of warship having various sizes and roles over a period of time. In the 17th Century, a frigate was any vessel built for speed and manoeuverability (Wikipedia). A frigate, in the main, is shorter in length than a destroyer but about the same width.

As I wrote before, I started work on a Blackwood class frigate for the Indian Navy in 1959 but progressed to the Taranaki, a year later.

I started work in F.O.B. as a fitter on board. This meant that when the empty shell of a ship was launched from the slipway at East Cowes, we fitters in F.O.B. were required to fit all the various pieces of equipment in the engine room, the Diesel Generator room and work on the Plumber Blocks (if a twin screw). The elephant's foot (support for the rudders etc) was fitted in dry dock at Southampton Dry Dock. Also on various other bits and pieces, like the boring out whilst on the slipway, for the stern tubes etc which I'll come to later.

Now my apprenticeship at J.S. Whites. Normally an apprentice fitter/turner would serve in two departments. The first department I served in was F.O.B. and should have been for 18 months. When I was 17½ years old, I was then expected to serve the remainder of my five-year apprenticeship – in machine shop.

Whatever department the apprentice ended his apprenticeship in would then designate, on becoming a fully-fledged Fitter/Furner, the trade he would work on. In short, I would become a machinist lathe operator. Except, I didn't!

You see, I had an altercation with a certain chargehand in machine shop. It really wasn't my fault, but this altercation nearly cost me my apprenticeship. To this *day*, I don't know how I avoided the sack. Here goes, this is what happened.

I don't know why, but as Yogi Bear would say, "You're smarter than the average bear, BooBoo." Unfortunately, I do seem to attract attention to myself without really trying – and this is what happened in machine shop.

The first six months, I was seconded to the Inspection part of machine shop, with was run by a Mr Reg Jackson. Now Reg was a right character and every day, without fail, he would come out with this little ditty:

*"Once upon a toyme*
*The bird shit loyme*
*And the monkeys, chewed tobaccy"*

Goodness knows why? But Reg was, for all that, a jolly fine inspector. I learned under his guidance how to use T.D.I.s (Test Dial Indicators), how to use Verniers, Leight gauges, micrometers, inside and outside calipers, stick-mikes etc. You name it, Reg could do it, as regards his knowledge of the tools required to check out the components that would enter his inspection bay to be vetted. He was a fair-minded man, and if a component was a 'borderline' case, he'd usually pass it and give the operator the benefit of the doubt.

After six months, my training in Inspection shop was at an end and I was introduced to a dilapidated-looking belt driven lathe, which looked as old as the factory itself. The lathe, with a huge-looking chuck, was in fact a machine for turning holding down bolts. On the day of the altercation, I was given the task of turning out about 80 holding down bolts, about a 1½" diameter.

Now to do this, the lathe operator, after tightening up the hexagon bar in the chuck, had to centralise each bar. This is done by allowing to turn the lathe at slow speed. As each revolution came around, then a 'lead' hammer would be used to correct the hexagon bar, which would be running out of true. The lead hammer consisted of a galvanised 2in pipe, which had a large ball of lead attached to the end of the pipe. Bang, thump, bang, thump, bang, thump.

Then it happened. Unbeknown to me, five or six apprentices had crept up behind me whilst I was pre-occupied with setting up the machine, and began to sing the 'Anvil Chorus' written by Verdi, for Il Trovatore.

Next moment, up comes the middle-aged chargehand, Stan Mumford. Stan is not a happy bunny when he sees what's going on. He then tears a strip off the 'choir' of apprentices and gives them short thrift, telling them to get back to work. Then he proceeded to lace into little old me which, I felt, was entirely unjustified.

By the time he'd finished telling off the other apprentices, he'd worked himself into a right old lather – in short, he'd completely lost it. His face was now apoplectic with rage. His face was beetroot red and after this, to me at least, unjustifiable outburst on *his* part, I lost it – the plot that is. Here was I, eighteen years old, a married man taking a load of garbage from an unfair-minded chargehand.

Suddenly, I snapped, throwing the lead hammer at Stan's feet, whereby he did a quick soft-shoe shuffle. I then shouted at him, "Well, stuff you, and stuff the job."

Do you know, Stan's face went from a bright shade of beetroot red to completely white. He didn't say another word. This was on the Wednesday morning. Then I thought, oh dear, what *have* you done John? You've stuffed up this time *big-time*!

Anyway, I worked my socks off on Wednesday afternoon, got to work early Thursday and Friday, had my toolbox opened up, and whatever tools I needed were on display, ready to be deployed for their usage. I finished the bolts on Friday afternoon, just before my shift ended, knocking spots off the time I was expected to complete them in. I believe by getting stuck in like I did, must have been my saving grace.

In mitigation to poor old Stan Mumford, we apprentices *could* and *were* a tough handful, especially with some of the stupid antics that used to take place. One mouthy git was tied up with his arms pinioned against his sides and hoisted up on a chain block and tackle – and left there for almost all of the hourly lunch break – about 15 ft off the ground. Happy days.

On the following Monday morning, before I'd had a chance to open my toolbox, a 'runner' from Stan Mumford told me not to unlock my toolbox but to return to F.O.B. where I resumed my apprenticeship – as a fitter – which I was *very* elated by. I've not spoken to Mr Mumford from that day to this, and I *still* don't know how I didn't get my marching orders. Chè sera sera – what will be, will be!

I started courting my wife-to-be, Marian, when I was eighteen years of age in March 1961.

We met in the Medina cinema in Newport on a Saturday afternoon. What was I watching? John Wayne, in "Rio Bravo". Early on in the film, I spotted two very attractive girls about the same age as myself. I chatted one of them up, as you do, and we hit it off straight away.

I can't remember much about the film as I was too occupied with other 'things'. In fact, I needed a second viewing of the film at a later date to get a gist of the storyline. In November 1961 we got married, and I've never regretted it.

Back to F.O.B. Although I'd been gone from F.O.B. for nine months or more, I soon slipped back into the routine.

I was now 18 years of age. Not one person queried my return from machine shop (I was virtually kicked out as an 'undesirable' addition to the machine shop, unfair, as in my mind, it undoubtedly was). I was over the moon regarding my return and vowed that I would more than make up for it. It was like being back home.

I was finally accepted as a would-be fitter, and was assigned to the Diesel Generator Room, complete with a labourer (or Navvy). At long last, I was in command of my own destiny and would sink or swim by my own efforts, so to speak. Certainly, I can remember waiting with a valve chest on a flat-bed trolley at the base of the hammer-head crane. Suddenly, my labourer shouted, "Get out of the way, fitter, that's my job," to get it craned aboard ship. That young man (I've forgotten his name unfortunately) really *did* earn his keep, saving me much wear and tear on the muscles. He was a big lad and seemed as strong as an ox.

With some help from Betto the chargehand who would advise me each step of the way, I was able to perform quite well and to the satisfaction of the powers that be. I do believe I'd redeemed myself in the eyes of supervision, who no doubt would have been monitoring my progress in light of my previous engagement – and demise – in Machine Shop!

At the time of writing, it's a bright sun-shiny day in the making, and, late for me, 8.30 in the morning. I am now 18 years old, going on 19, and have just embarked on another money-making exercise – by joining the Territorial army.

I now belong to the infantry division of the 4<sup>th</sup>/5<sup>th</sup> Battalion Princess Beatrice's 'B' Company on the Isle of Wight which is named by the street sign of Drill Hall Road.

As an 18-year-old apprentice, I was allowed to work two evening a week of two hours duration for each evening, and four hours of overtime on a Saturday morning. With time and a half (six hours total) and time and a third (evening overtime rate), it gave me an extra 11 hours pay a week approximately.

Belong to the T.A. I'd do the one evening a week training in the Drill Hall. On occasions, we would go to Newtown Ranges and with our trusty bolt-hatching .303mm Lee Enfield rifles, would have shooting practice at the targets down in the Butts (the name given to the target area).

I very much enjoyed that experience and was even being paid for the privilege of doing so. From time to time, the T.A. would have 'weekenders'. The weekender meant that we would leave the Island by army lorry on the Friday evening, not returning back until late Sunday afternoon. Not only was I paid three days money for the (almost) three-day weekend, but I was paid marriage allowance to boot!

Can't be bad, can it? Belonging to the T.A. as well as overtime at J.S. White's certainly made having to make ends meet much easier.

I absolutely loved being in the T.A. The camaraderie, the rifle training, the weekends, and surprise, surprise – the square-bashing. I simply loved the discipline of the marching, counter marching, the about turns, left, right turn, left wheel, right wheel. Dressing to the left etc, the sheer perfection that can be achieved when a group of soldiers are in step, are in union, and we are drilled into a competent body of men.

The drill sergeant was Sgt. John Dear and he took no prisoners, I can tell you. (I believe he died just a couple of years ago). As far as I am aware, Sgt. Dear was once in the British Army as a regular soldier – and it showed. He had quite a temper on him if things didn't quite go to plan. He wasn't a man you would wish to upset.

Sgt. Johnny Morgan was a tradesman like myself. He was a riveter by trade, with no army record as such (as far as I'm aware of). He eventually was to work in Saunders Roe (which eventually became British Hovercraft, then known as Westland Aerospace and ultimately G.K.N. Westland Aerospace).

Corporal Chris Beeney, and Corporal 'Bunny' Hutchings made up the administrative team. One weekender we went on was for promotional purposes when the BBC used Anita Harris in the photo shoots. The action took place in the New Forest I believe. There was another celebrity, who was made famous on the Hughie Green Show, and was quite popular with the men. She was big, blonde, busty and beautiful. Many of the lads clustered round her, like bees round the honey jar. One member of 'A' Company based on the mainland, a big strapping individual, was asked to carry her around, draped over his shoulders.

I felt rather sad about Anita Harris as very little interest was coming her way, yet she had more show business acumen than the blonde girl would ever have. But that's showbusiness as they say, isn't it?

J.S. White's sponsored the T.A. and agreed that they were happy to take an interest in allowing any of their employees to attend for annual Army Camp.

Although I've never been obsessed by the gun culture, the weaponry training that was given completely grabbed my attention. One exercise we used to do from time to time, at Newtown Ranges, was the 'Queen Mary Rundown'. We would start off at the 300-yard mark, in the prone position i.e. laying flat on our stomachs, propping up our .303 Lee-Enfield with one elbow supporting the muzzle of the gun. On the word of command, we would loose off 10 rounds of ammo at the target.

Once that was done, it was on 'safety catches' and we'd then run down to the 200-yard marker. On reaching the 200-yard marker, we'd then kneel on one knee, and be expected to loose off another 10 rounds at the target. Once we'd achieved that, we'd then run from the 200-yard marker to 100 yards from the target.

This next shot at the target was something else. After running for 200 yards with a full pack, trying to shoot the last 10 rounds with one's rifle waving around like a wand, this time it was to be a little more difficult. From the standing position, we had to try and put 10 rounds into the target. Fat chance of that, I can tell you. Fitness was the key to achieving a good score and controlling one's breathing when pulling the trigger. Hold one's breath, when about to fire etc.

We fired quite a variety of weapons during the four years I was in the T.A. My favourite was the Bren gun, also the Sten (semi-automatic), the S.L.R. (self loading rifle), the mortar and the mills grenade, and last, but not least, the Energer grenade.

The Energer grenade was like a miniature rocket. It was to be fired from a rifle by means of an attachment fixed to the nose of the rifle. The range of this grenade/rocket was approximately 75 yards – one's arm would be wrapped around the webbing (rifle strap) and you'd brace yourself to loose off the rocket in the manner I've just described.

Sometimes we would go to Brown Down, where weaponry training was given to us by the regulars from the British Army. One of the weekend jaunts was a beach landing on the island of Jersey, in the Channel Islands. That was a great weekend. I've even been picked to represent 'B' Company at Bisley, when rifle training, against other T.A. companies. All in all, the four years I spent in the T.A. were very enjoyable.

However, being inspected by Her Majesty The Queen at Little London was one of the highlights of my Territorial Army experience.

The icing on the cake, however, was performing the Trooping of the Colours at Broadlands in Romsey. This was an ancestral home belonging to Lord Louis Mountbatten of Burma. He held the position of Supreme Allied Commander, South East Asia Command. He was the last Viceroy of India and the first Governor General of independent India. From 1954 – 1959 he was the First Sea Lord. He also served as Chairman of the NATO Military Committee for a year. However, in 1979, he was assassinated by the Provisional Irish Republican Army.

But the pride I felt, as I marched around that parade field during the Drumhead Ceremony, was a wonderful experience.

Let's get back to basics, at F.O.B. Now there were two other trades under the same roof. Pipe shop (pipe benders) and the copper shop, which also bent pipes – copper pipes. It made perfect sense for these three trades (the fitters, the pipe shop and copper-shop tradesmen) to be under the same roof because we, the fitters on board, could keep track of the whereabouts of certain key components that needed to be installed first. This was in order that they weren't 'boxed in' by other pieces of equipment which could make fitting certain pipes an absolute nightmare.

How were these pipes made? What process was required in order to create what was required on the drawing?

First, the pipe-fitter would go out aboard, armed with a steel 'wire' usually a ¼" to 5/16" in diameter steel bar. He would carry with him also a 'bender' which was a steel bar with a ring of about ½" diameter, welded to the end. This bending tool would shape the wire, which basically would become a 'template' for the pipe that would eventually be 'copied' to the bends and the profile of the wire. Also, two wooden circular discs, the same size of the flanges that would eventually be welded (usually 'tack' welded initially) and finally finished off back in the workshop. The wooden 'flanges' or blanks would have holes in them so that a line of these wire templates could be hung from the pipe-hangers that would already be installed on board.

Once the line of wire templates for that system had been achieved, the system they were meant for would be replicated by the real thing back in pipe-shop (or copper-shop) as the case may be.

Bending the pipes was an art in itself, as they would be bent on a huge cast iron surface table. This surface table had numerous holes in it, approximately 4" or 5" in diameter. Large steel 'pegs' would be inserted in the required holes that would enable the pipe-bender to achieve his task. Extreme heat, supplied by an oxygen acetylene burner, would cause the pipe to glow red hot where the bend was to be actioned.

The most important piece of kit required at this stage of the game was a watering can of cold water. When the pipe was being pulled around the respective steel pegs, they were there to trap the pipe to keep it in place and to help form the bends in the pipe.

After a section of the pipe, still glowing bright red with the heat, was achieved, cold water from the watering can would cool it down where the bend had reached its ultimate shape, so that it could go no further. The shape of the pipe was replicated pretty near the shape of the template.

Once the pipe had been made, because it had to be longer than was required in order to facilitate its manufacture, the ends would then be cut off to the correct length. Only the steel flangers, complete with pre-drilled holes, needed to be affixed. This was done out aboard and the various flangers bolted together after being 'slid' on to the designated pipes – then 'tack' welded in the correct position. Later, the 'tack' welded flanges would be finish-welded in the workshop.

From time to time, dear reader, I will be relaying a true account of the skills that were needed to perform the tasks that we in shipyard had to overcome. I shall try to make these observations as interesting as I can, so please bear with me when I do.

Now that the flanges were finish-welded, all that was needed to be done now was for the welded flanges on the pipes to be surface-ground. They'd be suspended by a block and tackle in the required position and a huge surface grind-stone would be switched on, and the surface grinder would grind off the excess weld on the face of the flanges, so they (and this is where we apprentices first came in) could do the 'pipe-jamming exercise, outlined in one of the previous chapters.

Coming into the workshop from the direction of the hammer-head crane, on entering, one would be next to the tool-store to the right, immediately on entry. To the left, just around the corner, was the drawing store.

Now the drawings were all attached to a 'pole' usually about ¾" in diameter. They were wound round the pole, the drawings that is, and were made of fine Irish linen. In fact, from time to time, a drawing would become 'obsolete' before the items on the drawing could be fitted. This was because the latest piece of technology superseded what the previous drawing requirements were.

This was a bonus for us fitters, because being spanking brand new, the drawing was in pristine condition. Whether we were allowed to or not, we fitters, and I for one used to do it, would purloin the now defunct drawing, take it home (minus the wooden pole) and soak off all the emulsion in the bath. After washing, one would end up with a fine sheet of Irish linen!

Now I will mention the name of two fine young men who were welders. They were 'Plum' Cooper, and Fred Norris. These two herberts were amateur boxers and were based in Cowes. When a ship is first launched off the slip-way from East Cowes, it is virtually an empty shell.

Once it arrives and is moored on the Cowes side of the river Medina, then the shipwrights have to install 'deals' (two, side by side) to originate the walkways. The deals (planks of wood) were the only means of moving around the ship.

Being amateur boxers, 'Plum' Cooper and Fred Norris would sometimes hone their boxing skills by standing toe to toe, and 'sparring' with one another. One slip, and either of them would go down a hellava way to the bottom of the ship where the bilges were.

I wouldn't believe it, as Victor Meldrew would say. You couldn't make it up, but it truly did take place – I found it fascinating. They were lovely lads, they really were.

This is just one of the many things that I can recall from times gone by.

The Good Lord has blessed me with a very good memory and attention to detail, sometimes going way back in time. Some of the stupid things we as apprentices would get up to, one would find hard to believe. For instance, 'Ginger', a mouthy little 'git', was spread-eagled out on the wooden floor of the workshop, so we nailed him, by his overalls, to the floor. We put a cushion under his head and left him to extricate himself from this predicament. He had to rip the overalls he was wearing to shreds, in order to free himself. Happy days!

Oh, and just prior to that, one of the charge hands happened to come along, saw the lad laid out on the wooden floor, and kicked the cushion away that his head was resting on.

"Get up and do some work, you lazy little git, your hour's dinner break is over now." He then left him to do what he had to in order to get out of the mess he found himself in.

I've just recounted one of the stupid antics we apprentices used to get up to, about the lad nailed to the wooden floor by his overalls, but take note of the *next* incident concerning an apprentice.

'Chunky' was a 19-year-old apprentice, the same as me. The nickname 'Chunky' incidentally alluded to his build. Now this apprentice was working in one of the cabins close to the engine room. His job entailed marking off a place on the bulkhead whereby a pre-drilled and tapped plate (holes with threads in them) was prepared for welding to the wall of the cabin. Chunky had achieved that, managed to find a welder and the steel pad was now in place. *All* that was now required was a lick of paint (yellow chromate) to be applied to the newly welded pad or plate.

Next door to Chunky's cabin was a painter, complete with brush, simple, job done. Or was it?

Off trots the apprentice to politely request the painter's prowess (he was a skilled man, after all) to come next door to the neighbouring cabin to use his skill with his trusty paintbrush on the aforementioned pad, which was screaming for attention and a lick of paint. But no! Did the painter condescend to heed this apprentice's request? Not on your nelly!

Day two arrives, a polite request for the skills of that painter and his pot of paint, to be made manifest – but no! The request had fallen on deaf ears. Day three passes, with Chunky still twiddling his thumbs. You see, that welded pad was the start-off point for the rest of his job.

Attached to the pad was to be a valve. The flanges of the valve, once bolted on, would then allow the apprentices to bolt up a run of pipes on the system he was working on.

When the day had arrived on day four, 'Chunky' decided to take matters into his own hands. Armed with another brush from the stores, he waited until lunch break, which would have been an hour's duration.

When everyone was gone, he nipped into the neighbouring cabin, 'borrowed' the pot of paint – and painted the welded pad on the cabin wall. He took back the paint and obviously everyone else none the wiser, except *one* individual who copped what the apprentice has done and snitched as to what has happened to our skilled painter.

Oh dear, all hell appears to break loose, as the painter rounds up his fellow mates who promptly down tools. "Right, where's the stop steward," is the battle cry as this heinous crime, by an *apprentice* no less, has caused the line of demarcation to be crossed. "We're not having it lads, are we?" cry the deeply offended members of paint shop. "Where's the Convenor?" (The Convenor is the leader of the shop-stewards and he is now involved). The paint shop Convenor now goes head to head with our Convenor, the head of our union, the Amalgamated Engineering Union (A.E.U for short).

All this because of one man's pig-headed intransigence, who was too bothered to answer a request to do a two-minute paint job for three whole days, and more. How pathetic!

Chunky? He was given an undeserved 'rollicking' for nearly causing a strike and the anger of the paint shop crew had been assuaged. These paint shop 'brothers' couldn't take this incident lying down, could they. There was a principle at stake here – and they had made their point.

Storm in a tea cup? You bet your sweet life it was, but the lines of demarcation had been breached, hadn't they. 'Nuff said.

A few pages ago, I extolled the expertise of the skilled men in pipe shop and the ways and means of how they achieved the forming of steel pipes.

This time, copper shop and the means by which they achieved the same thing but with copper pipes instead. The bending into shape of 15mm and 22mm diameter copper pipes was relatively simple as springs could be used. A spring was a tightly coiled spring of solid looking proportion that could be slipped into the pipe to be bent.

It looked as solid as an iron bar but could be bent in any direction. Shallow or slight bends could be achieved by hand. However, the tighter bends would have to be done with the aid of a 'bender'.

The large pipes were a different matter. These would have to be 'blanked' off one end, and something resembling a 'bung' deposited in the bore of the pipe. Sand would be poured into the pipe via the opposite end, the pipe now being secured in the vertical position.

Once the pipe was full, in order for the sand to be 'tightly packed' a flat piece of wood was used to 'tamp down' the sand by continuously tapping the side of the copper pipe until the sand was a solid mass.

Once this was achieved, the second bung was inserted to seal off the end, to stop any sand from escaping. The pipe was now ready to be bent into shape. I believe a certain amount of heat was applied to facilitate the bending of the pipe.

There was, however, one big snag to bending copper pipes. The 'rippling' effect.

Unlike steel pipes, which keep their shape, copper pipes, on the inside of each bend, produce a series of wrinkles, which in some cases can be quite pronounced. These 'wrinkles' have to be 'dressed' out with the aid of a 'plannishing' hammer.

All day long, when these pipes were being made, the workshop would resound to the sound of these plannishing hammers as they dressed out all the imperfections caused by the bending.

Once the 'dressing-out' of all the parts that were required for this task was complete, the pipe would then be emptied of sand etc.

Once the achieved shape was completed, the bungs at each end were removed, the pipe now ready to have the flanges fitted.

In the time-honoured way, the flanges were assembled on the pipes out on board,, the main reason being, the flanges were pre-drilled and as such they had to 'marry up' to their respective neighbouring flanges of the adjacent pipes in the pipeline. Once again, the flanges would be 'welded' on, for want of a better word, and finished off back in the workshop.

# Chapter 6

*Tying Up Loose Ends*

In this chapter, I'd like to tie-up all the loose ends of my apprenticeship. As I mentioned in a previous chapter, I lost my temper with a machine-shop chargehand. However, I was also kicked out of Technical College, the reason being my lack of attendances because of the most important issue in my life. In short, I was courting my future wife at the time. With hindsight, perhaps I should have put my studies first and foremost, then allowed my courting to become secondary to the requirements in my life.

We apprentices had to take an entrance exam in order to 'slot' us in the required class at the Isle of Wight Technical College. I achieved quite high marks, and was placed in 'S1', the first year of the O.N.C. Ordinary Level of the National Certificate class – 'S1'.

Being eighteen years of age, and Marian of similar age, I messed up my schooling as required by the National Certificate Class by bunking off certain lessons to go to Newport town centre where I would meet up with Marian during her lunch hour.

When the exam came to decide whether I could go into Year 2 of the National Certificate course – I failed! Many of the lessons I had bunked off from were important to the passing of the exam. My non-attendance, unfortunately, caused me to mess up my technical college schooling. The result, I was 'demoted' to the City & Guilds class. Compared to the National Certificate class, City & Guilds was very mediocre, by comparison

Anyway, City & Guilds, for me, was an easy-peasy course. The Technical Drawing aspect of the first class of the day I absolutely loved. First angle projection, third angle projection, oblique projection, loved it. Achieving a three-dimensional shape by the use of certain techniques, wonderful. I simply loved the mathematical side of things. What now could go wrong? Answer – everything.

You see, I hadn't learned my lesson from my bad habit of bunking off lessons to go into Newport, to meet up with my future wife. The lessons I skipped were science and calculations. This second lesson of the day was more or less a repeat exercise of my last year of mathematical learning at grammar school. It concerned triangles, logarithms, sines, cosines, secant, co-secants, circles, triangles, hypotenuses and the like. I was bored. I had other things on my mind – Marian, and dare I say it again, Marian, and that was that. My time spent with Marian was more important to me, even if it jeopardised the academic side of my career. As Captain Mainwaring of Dad's Army would say, "You stupid boy." In reality, I was.

Anyway, what *did* put the cap on things was the taking of my City & Guilds exams. On a Tuesday evening I sat a two-hour exam. I completed my paper in one hour, handed it in, and on closing the door of the exam room with all the other students inside, I couldn't resist waving them all goodbye as I exited the room.

On the day of the second part of the exam – Thursday – I did the same again. Taking just under the hour this time, once again I left the exam room, casting a snook at authority with a cheery wave of the hand. All this, by the way, was duly recorded and my apprentice supervisor informed.

Because I'd missed approximately 20 Science and Calcs lessons, I was told by my supervisor my attendance at the Isle of Wight Technical College was no longer required. To cap it all, out of 12 apprentices, only four passed and I was one of them.

Even though I'd passed, I received a dressing down from the works manager, down to the chargehand and also the apprentice supervisor and I'd been kicked out of tech College to boot (please excuse the pun).
I'd like now, if I may, to take you on a tour of the two shipyards – because in reality West and East Cowes yards were as different as chalk and cheese.

Walking through the main walkway from Thetis Road gate: main stores for large items to be collected from and signed for to take a fit once on board; carry straight on and one would come across the 'pattern' shop. Great big wooden moulds or patterns were made specifically for the foundry. The foundry was sited on the left-hand side of the main walkway coming in from the main-gates close to the chain ferry.

Walking past the pattern makers, you would come to the sheet metal shop, for light alloy work; as often as not, the air ducting and cable trays. Also, all the cosmetic sheeting, whereby the bits and pieces fitted by the likes of F.O.B. for example, would have a bit of a facelift. The finishing touches by the 'sheeties' would make all our hard work 'presentable' by their expertise.

Carry on a bit further and eventually we would reach the hangar housing the lifeboats that were manufactured there.

Just before handing over the lifeboats, by the way, reminds me of the 'submersible' test. This involved the hammerhead crane, that would be employed to lift the lifeboat off the water in an upside-down position. When the desired height by which the lifeboat would be dropped was reached, the lifeboat would be released. This was done to test its self-righting properties. The time lapse that would elapse before the lifeboat became 'stable' and floating correctly would be recorded and written down.

Other departments on site at Cowes were the turbine shop and also boiler shop where they were made. Obviously, the offices near the entrance at the main gates from the chain ferry were in evidence too.

Talking of lifeboats reminds me of an event concerning a boat which used to take place on a daily basis. Glyn Davis and Cyril Blackwell (Blackie) plus four other mates, would row a skiff or large rowing boat from East Cowes sailing club to a point close by the lifeboat workshop.

Against the tide, it would have been heavy going. However they were all fit young men, and for them too it was a labour of love. Most of these lads from East Cowes sailing club would also have 'worked the line'. This meant that when sailing regattas, especially 'Cowes Week', took place they would act as marshals, virtually policing the events.

By that, I mean they would sometimes have to 'adjudicate' to decide who was or wasn't in the wrong concerning sailing etiquette, should there be a confrontation or altercation when two sailing vessels might clash. Penalty would be awarded against the offending skipper of the yacht that transgressed, or perhaps even disqualified, depending on the seriousness of the 'crime'.

Now I'm just about done, as far as the West Cowes half of Sammy Whites is concerned, except for a yearly event that would occur involving sea bass.

In the 1950s and 60s, on a yearly basis, the bass would appear. They would congregate at the mouth of the River Medina for one reason, and one reason only, for the white bait. White bait, incidentally, are the small fry of the herring family of fish (sometimes known as sprats). The sea bass would enter the river just before the turn of the incoming tide and lie in wait for the white bait. They, the sea bass, were so numerous their brown backs could be seen in their hundreds, as they turned to face the incoming tide – accompanied by thousands of white bait. There would be shoals, or schools, of them. The sea bass would have a field day when they arrived, the white bait were easy pickings for them.

This is where I would come in on the scene, armed with a fishing line (land line) complete with bass-hook – and a piece of silver cigarette paper from a fag packet. Often, there would be two vessels moored alongside one another, ideal for what happened next. During my lunch break (of course) I would lower my line from a porthole to land amongst the shoal of bass. On one occasion, I caught 16 bass, ranging from 1¾ to 2 pounds each in weight. I sold half of them to my fellow workmates and took the rest home. In short, a very enjoyable day's work.

Now for a study concerning the East Cowes site of Sammy Whites. Before I do, there is one topic that is very important. It concerns the impending crisis concerning the termination of Admiralty Orders for John Samuel White's, because of its inability, or refusal, to modernise the workshops. To be honest, the Admiralty Orders kept the yard solvent but the smaller vessels that would need running repairs of some shape or form, barely made ends meet.

I'm now approaching my fifth year of my apprenticeship, already there are whispers of redundancy. Now a law had been passed during my fifth year, that redundancy pay would be forthcoming to all those employed with more than two years' service, plus a week's pay for every year of employment. What did Whites do? They sacked all their shipyard workers on the East Cowes side, then re-employed them two weeks later. This meant that all the years of employment that could have provided a decent redundancy payment were no longer viable. By breaking their contracts, each worker would only have any redundancy payment from the renewal date of a new contract.

Sharp practice? You bet your sweet life it was. Did Whites have any choice in the matter? I honestly don't think the firm had enough collateral to pay the large sums of redundancy payment that they would undoubtedly have been responsible for. They, however, did keep going for a few more years before they folded which would end 200 years of Admiralty work!

Now finally, I would like to shed some light upon the practices of engineering on the East Cowes half of the shipyard. On occasions, the job of a fitter-on-board would take us to the other side of the river to carry out preparatory work and to facilitate the ongoing jobs that would be completed at a later date on the West Cowes side.

However, certain pieces of ironwork were sometimes necessary to carry out certain tasks more easily. These additions to our tool kit were as often as not forged in the blacksmiths shop over in East Cowes.

Take fox wedges for instance. These little beauties were forged from 3/8" thick flat bar, which would end up, after being forged, as a steel wedge 2" wide by 4"- 5" long, and tapering from zero to .375 (3/8") at the thickest end.

They would be used when setting up items of machinery, such as pumps etc, which would require steel packing on the four corners of it. The packers, after being measured up by the use of fox-wedges and small jacking bolts, complete with hexagon nuts, would 'set' the item of machinery to the required level. Regarding the thickness of the packers? Slip gauges would be employed on the four corners where each packer would fit, to ascertain the thickness of the four corners of each item. The packers would then be machined to the sizes obtained by the slip gauges. Obviously, the packers had to be plus or minus on the dimensions to stay in 'tolerance'.

Another very useful tool, forged by the blacksmith, was a 'podger' bar. This would have been forged by being heated up (being made from a ½" diameter bar) to a certain temperature and 'quenched' in water to harden it. Each end of the bar would be tapered slightly to 3/8" or slightly less. A 'set' or angle at one end would finish it off. What was it used for you may you ask? Answer, for lining up the holes of two 'mating' flanges, when bolting them together, after they had been 'faced', taken out on board, then finally fitted. A podger bar was a 'must-have' in any self-respecting fitter's tool kit, to realign the holes.

The third set of items – scrapers! These were forged from the many and varied shapes of files which, once being worn out through usage, could be adapted into the varied types of scrapers required by us fitters.

Half-round scrapers were made from 6" to 8" half-round 2$^{nd}$ cut files. These made very good deburring tools, especially on internal diameters of certain components, which needed dressing or filing, to make them fit for purpose.

The 'cow-mouth' scraper was something else. It became nothing else but a work of art, and actually, in appearance, resembled the look of a 'cow's mouth'. It would have been used primarily on 'white metal' bearing when 'lapping-in' the bearing to form as good a 'fit' as possible to the shaft, or object, the bearing was mated to.

A triangular file would be fashioned to make a 'riffler'. Used mainly for de-burring or 'fettling' metal components, the half round scraper, perhaps the most used of all the scrapers, was a more multi-purpose scraper.

Before I carry on with my accounts of life in the East Cowes side of the shipyard, I feel the need to put pen to paper concerning one warship that was built by J.S. White's. This was the Polish vessel Blyskawica. She was one of two ships built, and were G Rom Class Destroyers, the ORP Blyskawica and ORP Grom, for the Polish Navy.

On 4th and 5th May 1942, she helped to save Cowes and East Cowes from greater destruction than the deaths and damage caused by the worst air raid that the Island had ever faced.

It happened like this. The one overriding factor in all this, and why this warship of the Polish Navy was able to save the towns mentioned here, was because of one man's refusal to obey Admiralty Orders, which were to return all her ammunition back to stores whilst being refitted at Cowes. This man's name was Captain Francki.

On the 4th May 1942 at precisely 11pm, chandeliers of slowly descending parachute flares lit up the night sky. The residents of East and West Cowes knew that this was to be the 'biggie', the air raid of all air raids as far as they were concerned, and so it turned out to be. The bombers came in from the Solent, from the North, at sea level. The whole of J.S. White's dockyard was illuminated and Captain Francki ordered smoke candles to be lit, making a smoke-screen hiding the targeted area.

The destroyer left her moorings, heading directly at the attaching wave of aircraft, dropped anchor, and fired all its anti-aircraft weapons, forcing the bombers higher, reducing the accuracy of the bombing. The anti-aircraft guns fired continuously, the gun barrels growing so hot that the Polish sailors had to throw sea water over the barrels from buckets raised from the sea by hand, to cool the guns down. The ship fired in all 2,030 40mm Bofors shells and 10,500 rounds of machine gun ammunition.

If it had not been for the Polish Warship and its Captain, Captain Francki, the destruction in Cowes would have been much, much worse.

The facts of this account were obtained from The Hitchhikers Guide to the Galaxy: Earth Edition.

The two Polish vessels were named GROM (Thunder) and BLYSKAWICA (Lightning). Blyskawica is pronounced Bwi-ska-veetza, by the way. At this particular time in the war, these two destroyers were the fastest vessels afloat. At 114 metres (370ft) long they could reach speeds of 41 knots or more.

When escorting the Queen Mary to Britain carrying America troops, the Blyskawica was one of the few vessels capable of keeping up with her.

In 1940, the sister vessel of Blyskawica, the Polish vessel ORP GROM, was sunk by enemy action unfortunately. The Blyskawica is preserved as a museum ship in Gdynia and is the oldest preserved destroyer in the world.

Finally, I am coming to the end of my account of my life spent during my shipbuilding times at J.S. White's. I'd like to finish with a few accounts of what fitters on board were required to do, on the other side of the river.

I would enter the East Cowes yard straight off the chain ferry by going via the time-keeper's office. I'd be allocated a circular brass tally with a number on it. I would place the tally on the required slot on the board and retrieve it, about four hours later, in time for lunch break. The timekeeper duly logged what time I worked. Almost facing me would be the blacksmith's shop.

I don't know a great deal about the work of a shipyard blacksmith, but I suspect they had a hand in helping with the prefabrication of the large sub-assemblies that were welded in Falcon Yard, and some of the other work yards on the East Cowes site. Turning towards the right, I would walk past the large slipways that would eventually launch the ships at a later date. Then I would arrive at the main workshop at Falcon Yard.

Facing the river, the workshop didn't have sliding doors, or even any doors on that side of its building – only two huge tarpaulin like 'drapes' which served to keep the cold at bay. During the winter-time, especially frosty mornings, when working there it was as cold as charity. It was here the main sub-assemblies were produced.

On occasion, a white-metal bearing housing would need to be lapped-in, with the prop-shaft mounted on a special stand. The housing would be suspended from a block and tackle via two 'eyes' fixed to the outside of the bearing half. The shaft would have a light amount of blue marking dye spread along the area that the bearing housing would cover. The witness mark on the white-metal bearing would be scraped and finally finished off with very fine emery-paper and thin oil. 85-90% of the surface area would need to be achieved before it became acceptable to requirements. I quite enjoyed that job.

The second job was with a man I looked up to, Mr Eric Caws from East Cowes. Eric was a quiet, unassuming kind of individual who was very skilled at the next job I was allowed to help out on.

The job was the 'boring-out' of the stern tube of one of the Leander Class frigates. Because they were 372 feet long, during the very hot weather they could, because of expansion, 'bend' up to three feet up or down over its entire length.

Because of this, a 'witness' or height gauge, would be set up near the aft end of the vessel. This was done in order that the final cut of the day, from the 'boring-out' gear, was completed when everything had settled in the cool of the evening and was at a 'mean' temperature. The height of the gauge was marked in feet and inches.

I'll try to remember as accurately as I possibly can the procedure for the enlargement of the stern tube, to suit the size of the propeller shaft yet to be fitted (in dry dock at Southampton) at a later date. I was only 17 years old at the time, which was 60 years go. Anyway, here goes.

A piano wire was run from the boiler room, through the plumber block on to the stern tube, finishing at the 'A' bracket which lies aft of the stern tube. Once the prop shaft is coupled up to the 'A' bracket, the bit protruding out of the aft end of the prop shaft is the attachment point for the screw (or propeller).

A series of sight plates, square in appearance with a hole in a square plate held in place by four adjusting screws or bolts, held the piano wire as centrally as was possible. The adjusting screws were positioned at the four points of the compass. Two vertical screws moved the wire up or down, the two horizontal screws moved it from side to side.

Once the sight plates were all set up, then the measuring up of the stern to be could begin and the boring out gear (an antiquated looking piece of equipment if ever I saw one) would be brought into play. To centralise the piano wire, inside callipers would be used. Inside callipers were very similar to dividers, except that instead of them ending up being pointed, the ends of the two legs were slightly off-set. This off-set bit would be held against the bore of the stern tube and the callipers adjusted to 'flick' the piano wire ever so slightly. By doing this either side of the piano wire, then up and down in the vertical position, the wire would become dead central to the bore of the stern tube.

Now, the boring-out could start once the machine had been set up. Any discrepancies in the alignment of the rear stern tube would be corrected by the boring-out procedure itself. This accurate setting-up, measuring and boring-out was designed to eliminate any misalignment of the bearing surfaces that came into contact with the prop shaft. My job? As the apprentice, it was to stand guard over the turning gear (boring-out gear) with a 1½" brush, and to dip it into a large can of thick lubricating oil on each revolution of the lathe tool doing the cutting. Boring (in more ways than one) *but* it had to be done.

When the majority of the boring-out was done, one final 'cut' would have to be made. This would have been done before an Admiralty Inspector, approximately 8pm at night. This was when everything was settled down temperature wise. The amount to be machined, at this point in time, would be perhaps 20 thousandths of an inch – or slightly less. Job done!

None of the ship was actually built-up on the slipway. A large prefabricated section would be made in one of the workshops at Falcon Yard and lowered by crane into position on the slipway; each successive sub-assembly being added one step at a time, until the whole shell of the vessel was complete.

Once the engineering drawings were complete, it would take approximately a year to build the shell or structure of the vessel prior to launching and a further year to fitting out the engines, boilers, pipework. Then to dry dock for fitting of the 'elephant's foot' (the large vertical structure which carried the rudder) and various fitting out of the galleys, and obviously the telecommunication side of things, especially the anti-submarine frigates.

Well, I've just about come to the end of my apprenticeship at J.S. White's and very enjoyable and interesting it was too. Approximately seven months after coming out of my time as an apprentice, redundancy began to rear its ugly head. Before 'push came to shove' I applied for a job at Saunders Roe which eventually became B.H.C. then Westland Aerospace and finally G.K.N. Westland.

Working on aircraft and hovercraft was a brand-new ball game, and altogether, although I broke my service at Saunders Roe a couple of times, I did actually work there for a combined time of 37 years.

Before I move on and recall my journey through life at Saunders Roe, I'd like if I may just to say a few words about life at home and what had been happening during the last few years.

Marian and I moved out of 'Keepers Cottage' where she'd spent most of her life, to a flat in Bernard Road in Cowes. There lived an old lady, I've forgotten the old lady's name but she was a harmless old dear, well in her seventies, possibly early 80s. All she used to do would be to sit down in her armchair, whistling the same little tune, hour after hour.

Come 6pm without fail, she'd wander off to her local pub just down the road on the corner of Bernard Road. She would never buy a drink there. She would just sit – and wait. Sure enough, a well-wisher sooner or later would come up to her and say, "What're you having Ma?" She'd then request her customary milk stout.

The landlord used to turn a blind eye to the fact she would never spend even a brass farthing in his pub, but the locals didn't mind her presence there – she'd just become part of the furniture really.

Very infrequently, her daughter would visit her but as she lived in Scotland she didn't get to see her mother that often. One day, she decided her mum should update her gas cooker which was a bit of a nightmare for Marian and I. The old dear used to regulate her old gas oven by the height of the gas flame at the back of the oven. She was pretty good at it, too. But, and it is a big BUT, when she tried to do the same with her *new* oven, especially on a Sunday, the gas flame at the obligatory height she would set her new oven at, took her from one hour to nearly two and half hours to cook. She simply would not set her oven to number 6 or 7 on the dial.

Weekdays it didn't really matter, besides she'd be at least an hour in the pub anyway. We simply just had to grin and bear it, when Sunday came around.

Eventually, Marian fell pregnant again with another baby on the way. Once our baby was born, a little girl Kathleen, a sister for Caroline, it was only a matter of a few weeks and the council offered us a council house in Shorwell. It was way out in the sticks and beggars can't be choosers, can they? We moved out of Cowes and were to live in Shorwell for about eight years or more.

A couple of hours after we moved in, our next-door neighbour, Ivy Woods, brought round a beautiful homemade sponge cake complete with cream in the middle. Eric and Ivy Woods and their three children, Valerie, Leslie and David, were a lovely family. The Barnes lived on the other side of our semi. There was a good community spirit at Shorwell, a lovely village atmosphere. We happily settled in and our life-style was now a little more upmarket than what it used to be, in our one bedroom flat in Cowes.

One day, I decided to give Marian a treat. A friend of mine's Auntie had a cat that had given birth to a litter of kittens. Wally, my mate, asked me, as the kittens were now 10 weeks old, if I would like one. Without hesitation, knowing Marian's fondness for our feline friends, I said yes.

A few days later riding home on my motorcycle, I popped into his Auntie's house to pick up the kitten. Stuffing the creature inside my leather motorcycle jacket, I road home and knocked on our front door, and presented the kitten to Marian.

I wasn't expecting the response I received when I presented her with a feline friend.

"I've got my hands full with not only a toddler, but a baby that is being potty-trained, John. Now you've brought home a kitten for me to house-train when it does its business, nice one John. Well you can take it back."

"Oh come on Marian, look at its little face. He's taken to you already Mar, oh look at his little eyes Marian. He's only a little kitten."

"Well," says Marian, "he can stay outdoors then and become an outdoor cat then, for all I care."

"Oh Marian, please don't talk like that in front of the animal, he's starting to feel rejection now. Cats are very, very sensitive creatures Marian. These harassments of yours are really starting to get to him, his feelings are being utterly and completely crushed."

"Don't you try and sweet-talk me into accepting him – you didn't think to ask me John, did you, whether I wanted a cat? Oh no, act first and ask later, is that it?"

We kept the cat. Marian even named him Timmy. He grew into a beautiful shaped animal, long, lean and mean whereas other cats were concerned. He was predominately white with just a few black patches here and there. He had a lovely nature, even when the two girls tried to play with him. He just tolerated their behaviour and would simply walk away if things got a bit too hectic for him.

Timmy loved Marian, by the way, you could tell that, especially if it was a windy day when Marian would have to put the washing on the line. Simply put, Tim would 'ambush' her. He'd wait for Marian to walk round the side of the shed and cling on to Marian's legs and not let go. Marian had to put her wellingtons on when it was a windy day. The other place of ambush was at the side of the garden path, where he'd just spring at her.

All in all, Tim was my favourite cat out of all the cats we had over the years, about seven in all.

As often as not, we'd go on holiday to Butlins holiday camp at Bognor Regis leaving Mrs Woods, our neighbour, to feed the cat. On our return on Saturday afternoon, there was no sign of Timmy. Anyway, after fruitless searching and banging of tins of cat food, still no joy. On Sunday, I went looking for him and found him three fields away near Woolverton Manor farm. He wouldn't let me stroke him. He had a bit of a cob on and pulled his head away. He did, however, condescend to let me pick him up and carry him home to Russell Road.

I took him indoors and no, even Marian couldn't stroke him either. Then, inexplicably, he just rushed upstairs emitting what must have been a loud cry of anguish as he charged around the bedroom. It was nearly a week before he 'came round' and settled back into his old ways. He was a character, he really was.

A couple of years down the line, we were asked to look after my workmate's cat, Dave was the workmate at Shorwell Plant Hire Co at Bowcombe, for a week. The cat's name was 'Simba' (it means 'lion' in one of the African languages). This cat was a long-haired black creature – with attitude. One day, I sat down next to the window in the dining room, when Marian screamed "Look out John" as I moved away from the window. Simba was behind the dining room curtain, saw me, and was, with his talons fully extended, attempting to have my eye out.

You see, Simba's owner had a ten-year-old boy who just wouldn't leave the cat alone. To cut a long story short, Marian took a shine to the cat, and Dave was quite happy to part with the animal.

One day, and I'll finish with this, Timmy and his new-found 'friend' had a fight. There was black fur and white fur everywhere. To cap it all, both leapt into the air at one another, and I swear for just a second or so they were both locked in an airborne feline embrace. I was fascinated by this demonstration of aerial acrobatics by both animals. Marian shouted at me to get a jug of water. I mean, this was a cat fight, to end all cat fights, *but* the jug of water *was* necessary to cool them down and, seeing what was coming before I hurled the water over them, they parted company, acrimoniously, in order to live and fight another day – bless 'em.

Marian and I both loved living in Shorwell. It got its name, by the way, because the well at Northcourt Manor house, never, ever ran dry. It was a 'sure' well, later to become known as Shorwell, giving its name to the village. (True story that).

Our road, 'Russell Road', was named after the Russell family who ran a farm next door to Woolverton Manor Farm. They were a Christian family and Geoff and Joy were very good friends of ours. 'Nutty' Edwards ran the 'Crown' at Shorwell and village life was absolutely sublime. The kids went to the local primary school at Shorwell; the village had its own grocery shop complete with Post Office facilities and the Doctor's Surgery was just up the road, about half a mile away in Limerstone (halfway between Shorwell and Brighstone).

I joined the local football team at Brighstone and would train once a week on their ground. Living in a small village, for me, was idyllic. I was now 22 years old, with a lovely council house, a lovely wife, and blessed with two pretty young daughters, only twelve months or so separating the two girls ages.

I could come home, forget about work and concentrate on the garden. There was 40ft of lawn at the front of the house, and approximately 100ft of garden at the rear. Most of that, apart from the first 25ft of lawn, I managed to put to good use, planting vegetables.

This is where Marian's Dad came into the equation. He would come up on his 125cc two-stroke motorcycle and say something like, "Okay my boy, I've got some cabbage plants enough for two rows. Dig enough to plant them, I'll bring them here in a week's time."

Before leaving for work at 7.15am in the morning, I would be up at 6.15am and, weather permitting, I would dig about two spits along (two rows) and doing that by the second day of digging, there would be more than enough of the garden ready for planting.

The same with runner beans. You see, Dad was the head gardener at Whitecroft Hospital. His greenhouses were his domain and some of the inmates, it was a mental hospital after all, would sometimes help out Dad by weeding and tending the plants.

All I had to do was to stay ahead of the game and ensure the ground was ready for whatever Dad was growing at the time.

"Right my boy, I've got some powder here, permanganate of potash. Sprinkle some around the perimeter of the hole, prior to planting. It'll make a lotta difference to your crops."

In those days I was fit, with circuit training on the football field once a week, Wednesday usually, and overtime two evenings a week plus four hours Saturday morning. I had to be, didn't I.

My first department at GKN was fitters forty (from now on I shall lump together Saro, BHC, Westland Aerospace as one – GKN – it makes life much easier).

The only drawback with living out in the sticks was transport, or *lack* of it. No bus leaving Shorwell could possibly get me to East Cowes. At the time and at age 22 years told, it was either by pushbike or on my old 250cc BSA C11g. Alas, it had seen better days but at the time it was all I could afford.

One day the darn thing blew a head gasket. I had to go on my pushbike to Newport, put a padlock and chain on the thing and park it in the lane between St Thomas' Square and Southern Vectis Bus Station.

Fitters forty (what a name) was derogatively given to the department where I suppose an average of 40 detail fitters worked there. Some fitters who were transferred there absolutely hated it there, as the work, making 200 of this, 100 of that, 25 of the other, could be monotonous and, I suppose, boring.

However, I loved it. Why? Because, whereas working practices after five and a half years became second nature, the work at GKN was a brand-new ball game. I was virtually learning a new trade from scratch; it was akin in a way to searching a new apprenticeship. This time, however, I was paid a skilled man's wage.

This period at GKN was the onset of the hovercraft era. In my last year at White's, as often as not, I'd see a round-looking object, about 15 feet in diameter, whizzing around concreted areas outside the Union Jack gates of Columbine shop, facing the sea. This was the prototype of SRN1, invented by Sir Christopher Cockerell. GKN then went on to make the SRN5, SNR6 hovercrafts (the ones that travel from Ryde to Southsea each day) also the N4s and various others, for the military etc.

On the odd occasion, supervision would ask us fitters to work a 'ghoster'. This meant that when we finished our normal day's work at 5pm, by law we had to take two hours off for a rest period then resume work at 7pm, working right round to 6am the following morning, taking 30 minutes off for lunch break. When travelling 10 miles or so to work and 10 miles back again, it could be a dangerous business. I remember a painter in paint shop, who lived at Freshwater, was driving home from GKN one morning, fell asleep at the wheel of his car, hit a tree – and died instantly.

This became a sobering thought and there but for the Grace of God, go I.

I'd now left the Territorial Army after learning to be a trained solder, and being paid for it, too. So, I'll first relate one of the wilder escapades of yours truly whilst on a weekend jaunt, a three-day-er as it happened.

The 4th & 5th Battalion was awarded at Winchester the Freedom of the City. This was an honour and meant the Drums & Bugles led by Bandmaster Urry, resplendent in their dress uniforms, looked a picture, we in the infantry bringing up the rear.

On Saturday night the lads decided to go on a bender and let their hair down, so to speak. We decided to have a few bevvies of beer then go for a Chinese meal and back to the drill hall to bed down for the night. Now, I *should* have seen this coming, but I didn't. Ray, one of the bandsmen, whipped off my beret and said he was having a whip-round, as I protested vehemently.

Now you don't argue with someone like Ray, if you know what's good for you. I mean, he's built like the proverbially brick-built outhouse, and being a runner-up at the A.B.A. boxing final, he was a force to be reckoned with. After a drink or three, Ray was virtually unstoppable. In fact, after forcing the younger 17-year-old bandsmen onto their knees and made to pray on one occasion (this was once at Army Camp), it took five of us to restrain him when he wouldn't settle down. One man on each arm, one on each leg, and 15½ stone Drummy Urry to sit on his stomach. It took ten minutes before the fight went out of him, then he fell asleep.

But once again, I digress. The whip-round, you guessed it, was for me. Now I only even drank lager shandies. Usually a couple of small shandies would last me all evening. Don't ask me why? But drinking whisky Macs and Guinness I found abhorrent. People actually put this stuff down their necks – and enjoyed it? Not for me. Soon there was a pint of shandy next to my first drink. Come on Bootsie, drink up, you've got to finish this one as well, you know.

With all this booze, I started to go to the loo. Each time I returned from the toilet there was <u>another</u> pint shandy waiting to be supped. Unbeknown to me, the whip-round was paying for the vodkas being entered into my drink. By 9pm my body knew where it wanted to go, but my legs wouldn't respond. Sometime later, we made it to the Chinese Restaurant but I felt rather dozy and my recollection from there on was rather sketchy.

To cut a long story short, I ended up being draped over somebody's shoulder and being unceremoniously carried back to the Drill Hall. Then, things took a turn for the worse. One of the younger members of the band started to take the mick. Now by this stage of the game, I couldn't have punched my way out of a paper bag but, undeterred, I decided to teach the young whippersnapper a lesson. Crash, bang, wallop – no, not me – but the whole row of bandstands went flying in my determined, but ludicrous pursuit of sorting out this young pipsqueak.

Then, three of the lads took matters into their own hands.

"Are you going to bed down for the night, Bootsie, or are we going to make you".

"You and who's army?" I snarled back. Then something connected with my chin, I saw stars, momentarily, and was in the land of nod. They'd knocked me out, bless 'em.

After four years with the T.A. I decided to leave. Unlike the regular army, where you signed up for a number of years and if you prematurely wished to leave would have to buy yourself out of the British Army, with the T.A. it was voluntary and therefore different.

A year later, aged 23 years, something remarkable took place. I became born again (of the Spirit of God). Although I'd now been married to Marian for five years, she never, ever spoke of her time at Sunday School; of a certain visit to Wembley Stadium, and at 12 years old, at a Billy Graham Crusade, giving her heart to the Lord Jesus Christ and allowing Him to be her Saviour.

Two Christian Heralds, who were Bible students at Moreland Bible College, came knocking on the door and spoke to Marian who re-dedicated her life to the Lord.

In the Isle of Wight County Press, a Crusade was being advertised, for a week at a little Mission Hall at Pallance Road, Northwood. Marian wanted us to go. Reluctantly, I got out the motorbike and, with Marian riding pillion, we arrived there to be greeted by the Thomas family and the Evangelist John Wyre and his evangelistic team of helpers.

There were about 60 people at the meeting and I was quite taken by the Evangelist, John Wyre. You see, since early childhood, I had attended Sunday School until the age of 13, when I attended the Church of St. Edmunds at Church Road, Wootton. The last time at morning assembly at Newport Secondary Grammar, was when I left school to begin my career as a fitter/turner.

Now the aim of this book is, I hope, to write a book that is entertaining, factual and which gives an account of the various milestones I was privileged to accomplish. I don't intent to go on a Bible-bashing campaign, but, as and when I have something of a Christian viewpoint to express, then so be it.

I am very aware we live in a multi-cultural society with many, many religions being practised.

So, at that John Wyre meeting, I realised I knew everything *about* Jesus but I didn't know him in a personal way, like the Evangelist. Because of my upbringing and circumstances beyond my control, I never had a father figure in my life. My grandfather certainly never fitted that role. Do you know friends, I suddenly realised that God is real, Jesus is real and I honestly felt the presence of God there as I gave my heart to the Lord and accepted Him as my Saviour.

Mr Thomas and his wife Iris welcomed us to church and Pastor Thomas would drive from Cowes to Shorwell to pick us up and ferry us to Church every Sunday. We shared a Sunday dinner in Beckford Road, where the Thomas' lived at that particular time.

An old gentleman, in his late 60s perhaps, would preach on a Sunday morning as often as not. This is <u>his</u> testimony. During the first World War, he served in a Hampshire regiment on one of the major battlefields. It was trench warfare, and there came a time when a blast on a whistle was to signal for he and his comrades to leave the safety of the trench and 'go over the top', crossing the terrain known as no-man's land. He said, "8 out of 10 of my comrades were either shot to pieces by the German guns or were wounded. I cried to God. I didn't even know how to pray, but it went like this: 'God, you get me out of this mess God, safe and sound, so that I can get back home to my home in Blighty, back in Sandown on the Isle of Wight, God – and I'll serve you for the rest of my days on this earth."

When the time came, he did return back to Sandown and he honoured the agreement he made with Father God.

When Mr Dimmer preached, it would always be about something of interest in the Old Testament. He would *always* apply the Old Testament to the New and would give the appeal. His face shone with God's Glory, and he certainly knew Jesus as his Saviour. To him, God was real, Jesus was real and God's Holy Spirit was very evident in his life. He was a lovely Christian man, he really was.

# Chapter 7

## *Moving On – Germany and GKN*

This chapter concerns the working practices of fitting shop, which was on the balcony above Columbine shop, the one with the Union Jack flag painted on it.

Many years before, when I was just a young lad, I can remember a Princess Flying boat tethered over at Cowes next to the chain ferry office and almost opposite the entrance to J.S. White's. She seemed huge. In fact, the tail plane sub-assembly could not be fitted in the hangars because of its size – there simply wasn't the height to pre-fit the tail assembly in-house. It had to be done outside, which presented of itself a challenge. But, although a beautiful looking aircraft, the engines were not really man enough to quickly get the airplane 'airborne'. We could have done with some practical assistance from the Americans but none was forthcoming. I suspect that because this aircraft was ahead of its time, the Yanks, because it wasn't *their* baby, didn't *want* to know how to improve its performance.

Over the years at GKN, I worked on many aircraft, hovercraft, helicopters and even a spell in fibre-glass shop in 1975, after I'd broken my contract with GKN I had gone contracting in West Germany on three separate contracts at Augsbug M.A.K. in Friedricksort on the Kiel Canal, and Donauwörth in Bavaria.

Was it God's providence that I went to West Germany to work as a connie (contractor)? All I know is that in 1973 when I was aged 30 years, I swapped council houses for one in East Cowes. Within two months, when going to view a second-hand carpet which John, the deputy convenor was selling, I ended up with his house. Yes, his house. I had no deposit for a house, so John loaned me £900 as a deposit.

Northwood House, a Tory controlled council, were selling council houses in order to better balance their books financially. Once sold, a council house cannot be a burden on the council can it?

We were granted a mortgage because of the deposit we now had. To cap it all, three of my fellow workmates had made contact with a representative of an engineering agency inviting people to become contractors, the money being twice what the Germans were getting and apparently four times the take-home pay of GKN. John, Charlie and Cyril were all riveters and said to me, this was on a Saturday, "Come with us Bootsie. We'll tell the rep and you can fly with us by next Saturday." I consulted with Marian and we both felt it was the right thing to do.

I went contracting with my fellow workmates and joined them on the Lufthansa flight to Munich. From Munich, we caught the train at the bahnhof to Augsburg, then by tram to the Prinz Leopold, a hotel for want of a better word, to the connies. We had arrived to work at Messerschmidt, Bilcov-Blohm complete with an ME 109 tethered on the front lawn.

I loved contracting, I really did, especially in Germany. You see, I'd studied German as one of my O Level GCE subjects and although my apprenticeship was to prevent me taking my 'O' Levels, three years of learning German did me in really good stead for my new job. The factory at Augsburg, was bombed and strafed during the war, and the cannon shell holes in the vertical 'H' beams still bore the signs of that conflict.

Contracting can be a hard life and Marian would write to me virtually every day. I tried to keep up with her writing to me but ten-hour days and six hours on a Saturday morning, as often as not, took its toll.

On occasions, and I'm not ashamed to admit it, when on my own I'd shed a few tears. I missed my wife and kids and since our marriage in 1961, this was the first time that Marian and I had ever lived apart. But you just pick yourself up, dust yourself down and soldier on regardless.

I took my Bible with me, which was a comfort, but being in isolation virtually, with nobody else of a Christian standpoint, made my spiritual well-being difficult. I was separated from Charlie, Cyril and John because their digs had already been sorted out for them. Me, I had to fend for myself as best I could.

One day, Gerry Sims, a Catholic lad from Northern Ireland, invited me to join their hostel in Königsbrün (which means Kingstown). His brother Patrick owned an Audi Saloon car and if I was prepared to pay a little towards the petrol, so be it.

Altogether I was eight months in Augsburg on that contract.

Now because work was starting to 'dry-up' to a certain extent the contract was being run down, and we contractors were alas becoming few in number as the person in charge thinned us out.

I was employed as a 'sheetie' in Germany. I did have a small amount of knowledge of sheet metal work and managed to make the grade.

The person I give my appreciation to is a man by the name of Ray Thomas. He taught me, in fitters forty back at GKN, how to roll a piece of aluminium in preparation for the salt bath (to soften the material for approximately two hours) to make it workable; how to work out the angles for the folders. He showed me the ropes concerning the usage of 'shrinkers' and 'stretchers' when forming angles to fit the curvature of, say, the bow section of an N5 or N6 hovercraft.

I learned and now I was able to put those skills to good use in West Germany, all down to Ray. No wonder he ended up in charge of the renovation of second World War aircraft at Sandown Airport, not far from Morrisons, near Lake. He was a very good 'teacher' in the art of sheet-metal work and I am eternally grateful for his ability to demonstrate and pass on those skills to other people. Spitfires and Hurricanes became second nature to his skills and once again, at Sandown, he was a guiding light.

M.A.K. an engineering works at Friedricksort, was my second contract in West Germany. Friedricksort was the place that a custom-built sailing centre became evident during the Olympic games one year.

Be that as it may, I joined the firm as a driller but I didn't bargain on the sight that greeted me when I turned up for work on the first day of my employment. For some reason, being a driller, as far as I was concerned, was standing at the front of a pillar drill. I thought easy-peasy this job will be. *No.* The drill in question (and I suspect because I was a connie) was the biggest radial arm drill I've ever seen. I said to Hughie, the company rep, "This is a new ball-game for me pal. I've never worked on one of these beasts in my life."

"You'll be all right John, the Germans won't let you mess up. Besides you're a quick learner anyway John, you'll survive."

I thought, well I'll get a month's pay out of it before they kick me out anyway, so I'll just have to give it a go.

I did master that machine, and the German 'Capot' was pleased with my progress. He could only speak a few words of English, the main ones (honest Injon) were "Johan, here we go round the mulberry bush".

My command of German, although I say it myself, was far more knowledgeable than his command of the English language. Between the two of us, we got by, and we had the occasional laugh, about, for instance, England's prowess (or lack of it) against their German football team.

Now Hughie and I shared a top floor flat in a hostel sponsored by M.A.K. It was no great shakes as a flat although it was clean enough. To reach it involved walking up a metal staircase, on the outside of the building. One night at about 11pm, above the landing, one of the Germans, because he was too drunk to know what he was doing, tried to get in via the skylight. He didn't make it. In fact, because he weighed approximately 14 stone, he shattered the skylight, dropped on the landing. His wife was at home but with the absence of the outdoor key to the landing he couldn't have got in.

His Hausfrau knocked on my bedroom door. Her husband was bleeding profusely but she wouldn't call a doctor, could I help? The only material I had was from a pair of long-johns, which were clean, and reluctantly I tore them into strips vaguely resembling bandages, cleaned up his wounds best I could and bandaged him up.

You'll need stitches." "Nicht gut", das ist nict rihtig, sie muss ein Doktor sehen, Montag jah?"

Roughly translated, "Not good, this isn't right, you must see a doctor on Monday, yeah?"

But he was happy with the way I'd patched him up and when 'Montag' came round he was off to work, long-johns and all!

From Friedricksort, I was offered another contract to work in Donauwörth. The word 'Donau' by the way is Deutsche way of spelling the name of 'Danube' so 'Donauwörth' was the word for 'Danubetown'.

This firm made post-office wagons. I was paired up with a young German lad just a little younger than my 30 years. We got on well together. The vertical supports the structure was made from, after welding the steel sheets on, would end up 'bowed' like a banana. It was our job, with the aid of an oxygen-acetylene burner, to heat up these vertical supports (like miniature 'h' beams really).

After they were heated, it was sledgehammer time with a 'swage' on a long handle starting at the bottom. The person holding the swage, similar but smaller obviously than an anvil, would move the swage up six inches at a time, whilst the person with the sledgehammer would give it a heavy whack before moving the swage up another six inches.

After beating ten bales of sugar out of the job, usually it took three goes at it, checking with a straight edge before moving on the next pillar or support, that part of the job was done.

The boring bit came next when, with the disc grinder, the welding marks had to be made flush. It was hard work but the time went quickly though. I originally stayed at a dear hotel, called the 'Schwartze Adler' which means Black Eagle.

What I *did* learn to play was a guitar, when I was in Königsbrün, near Augsburg; my first song 'Grain of Sand', self-taught. I did master it – eventually!

This next piece of dialogue concerns bullying in the workplace. Now I've always fought my own battles when I had to and usually came out on top. But one idiot at GKN couldn't or wouldn't keep his hands away from my upper arms. At some point in the day, he'd punch me hard on the upper arm muscle against the bone. He did it to goad me into retaliation. Why, I don't know. All is know is my arms were black and blue with the hammering he used to give me.

Because I'd become a Christian and was also a Deacon and part of the Deaconate of the Ryde Elim Church at Albert Street, fighting in the workplace wouldn't have been, and would not have presented, a good image to the world. Eventually he emigrated to Australia with his wife and family.

One of my workmates got married, inviting all of the other lads to the wedding and he pointedly told him he wasn't welcome because of his bullying ways with me, and so he didn't get an invite.

I'll share this little story, which is relevant to the situation I was in. Horatio Hornblower was a sea captain, who challenged a nasty piece of work who'd violated a woman friend, to a duel. With pistols drawn at dawn, back to back, the two men walked the ten paces before turning to face each other. Before the command 'fire' was given, Hornblower's adversary discharged his fire-arm – and missed. Grovelling, he begged Hornblower for mercy. Hornblower looked at the man and said, "You're not worth the powder" and fired his gun into the ground.

The bully boy at GKN, after emigrating to Australia with his wife and kids, left his wife and kids for an Australian Sheila. He deserted them. I've not mentioned him by name because in the words of Horatio Hornblower, frankly, *he's not worth the powder!*

Anyway, back to GKN. After 1975, when I came back home with my contracting days now over, I applied for a job and returned to a new shop called fibre-glass department, under a right character of a foreman known as 'Lofty Argyles'.

He knew his job, was a little eccentric in his behaviour, but for all that was quite a clever man. The job was okay but wasn't fitting, in the true sense of the word, but it paid the bills.

Eventually I got a transfer to the fitting shop (sub-assembly shop) making the Britten Norman Islander sub-assemblies. Building an aircraft isn't so very different from building a model aircraft kit only much bigger, but the principles are the same. We built the cigar-box structures, which were the wings of the aircraft minus the leading edges, the rounded part on the front of the wing and the trailing edges. We built the structure then skinned it after the structure was cleared by inspection.

I also worked with Reggie Barnes on the tail plane. Reg was a very good airframe fitter and I learned a lot from him. After the Islanders came to an end, I worked on the Lynx helicopters and eventually on to the Gazelle join-up. That was a brilliant job for me.

One of the best contracts at GKN was the Centre Wing for a firm called 'Short's of Belfast'. We had four jigs and could turn out four of these 'Short's wings' a month.

One of the fitters I had the pleasure to work with was a character by the name of Spike Gaudian. Spike is no longer with us as an inoperable cancerous growth, that the doctors had missed for seven years, finally caught up with him. Unfortunately, I was unable to attend his funeral. We used to work on nights together at fibre resin department in Clarence Road, East Cowes. He used to be a right storyteller and here is one of them.

"One day Bootsie," he said, "we did something about the camel drovers." This was whilst on a working party in Saudi Arabia, retrofitting some components that hadn't arrived when it was being manufactured in England, on the Island.

"What happened then Spike?" I asked.

"What happened?" says Spike, "I'll tell you what happened," replies our disgruntled fitter.

"Every morning at first light these blooming camels with their drovers, would come to the drinking troughs before they set off on their journeying across the desert at 5 am in the bl...y morning, so we did something to their drinking water."

"You mean you 'spiked' their drink then mate?"

"Did *we*?" he replied. "We brewed up a strong brew of senna pods and poured it into their drinking water."

"What happened next then Spike?"

"What happened, what happened? If you had drank a load of senna pod 'tea' like what they drank, you'd be beside yourself with the back door-trots, wouldn't you?"

The camel drovers didn't know what to do. Their animals were emitting the most terrible stench and were leaping around spraying everything in sight. One car, parked up fairly close to the drinking trough, was so badly pebble-dashed with their effluent that its owner really laced into the camel drovers, who were completely at a loss as to why their animals were behaving in this way. I mean, they not only pebble-dashed the car but sprayed each other as well. Those camels and their handlers were a sorry sight.

Spike says, "That's what happened, 'cos I was there."

Now the next story *is* true according to John's wife. Back in Guernsey, when John was about 11 years old, he and some other kids going to school, would grow in numbers as they met up with children from the various farms dotted about along the way.

One day, on reaching one particular farm, the old Shire horse had dropped dead.

"Brown bread he was," says John. "Brown bread."

"What happened next then Spike?"

"What happened?" he echoed, "I'll tell you what happened – what happened was we buried him, that's what happened."

"A Shire horse is a big horse Spike, isn't it?" I said.

"Well, with about twenty kids all mucking in and a small mechanical digger doing its stuff, in twenty minutes the hole was dug."

"How did you bury it then mate?" I asked.

"Well, we rolled it into the hole where it landed on its back, but there was a problem."

"What d'ya mean, a problem?" I countered.

"Well, with rigor-mortis setting in, its legs were sticking straight up in the air," says Spike.

"What did you do then mate?"

"What could we do, we sawed off its legs, chucked them into the hole, and carried on filling in!!"

Now for the serious business, building aircraft, especially the Short's Wing, the 'centre wing', as we would call it. Once again, this involves John.

In my opinion, having worked with him on night shift for a year or more, John was one of the fastest workers I've had the pleasure to work with.

It was our job on night shift to work on the spar ends after a day shift had loaded the front and rear spars into the build jig. It was a good night's work as it was precision engineering and the jig pins that were used to set up the spar ends had to be fitted so they could be withdrawn easily.

The spacing between the front spar and the rear was a 'toleranced dimension' and had to conform to the requirements of the Inspection checks. The drilled and reamed holes had to be in accordance with the 'go' and 'no-go' gauges that were used by Inspection to pass the job off as being of an acceptable standard. This we both achieved on a regular basis because it had become routine procedure and became almost second nature to us.

No matter how hard I tried, John *always* finished his ends about an hour before mine. Sometimes he'd toy with me, I'm sure of this, and would shilly-shally around at the commencement of the shift and virtually give me an hour's head start - and still finish first. He had too much pride to allow things to be any other way.

Because John only had one lung because of a motorcycle accident in his youth, you would have thought he'd be impaired because of it, but no, it didn't affect him in the least.

John was always a bit of a rebel and the next account of John's way of dealing with a 'problem' epitomises this. For months, John had been belly-aching to supervision about a fitting that didn't quite 'marry up' to the pre-drilling of the spar, 'pilot holes' that were already there to facilitate the operation of setting up the job.

But on *one* plate on the rear spar (Spike's end naturally) the pre-drilling was out. The plate that was pre-drilled didn't conform. John decided to drill off this plate on which we'd had to spend approximately an hour's work to overcome the problem. As far as Spike was concerned, enough was enough. John scrapped the skin deliberately! He knew, that without dragging the holes and messing about with all that malarkey, what would happen.

John was in the dog-house. 'Rolfie', the foreman, went bananas. Was John phased by all this? Not a bit of it, he'd now graphically brought to supervision's attention a problem that had never been addressed for a couple of years. Did supervision act on this? You bet your sweet life they did. The remedy? Leave out offending pick-up holes on the build stage of the spar so that the problem was eliminated.

John taught supervision a lesson the hard way. Hook or by crook, he'd proved his point - and the job was now easier to do. This was the 'rebel' coming out in him. The scrapped skin? While 'Rolfie' was away at a board meeting for three hours, John drilled off the old skin, fitted *and* riveted the new replacement skin, and got the job back on track.

John was a one-off. When they made him, they broke the mould. He would speak to the foremen and managers the same way that he would speak to the likes of you or me. It wasn't that he was being disrespectful, it was just that he considered himself to be co-equal, if not *more* knowledgeable than the hierarchy of upper management who employed him.

One day, he decided to apply for a chargehand's job. Now to do this, you first must have the approval of supervision, in this case 'Rolfie'.

"What makes you think Spike, that you'd be good enough to become a chargehand?"

Quick as a flash, Spike replies, "Well, they made you a bleedin' foreman, didn't they?"

Rolfie put John's name forward anyway. Needless to say, Spike didn't get the job, 'surprise, surprise'.

John was always clowning around. If there was a group of people around and John was amongst them, he would be centre-stage. John (Spike) just didn't conform to the normal scheme of things. He and his wife lived in one half of the HP house at Binfield Corner. He kept exotic animals, one of which was a Cayman, a type of small crocodile. He only got rid of it because it grew too big for the bath.

I could write a book about John's life-story, I really could, but I must move on with the rest of my own memoirs.

Not only did we just fit the spars but John and I would fit the frames and intercostals etc, and all the details such as gussets, corner pieces and stiffening angles.

Then after riveting we'd skin-up the structure. After delivering and wet-assembling the skins, the riveters would do their job, then the most boring job of all would have to be done. The countersunk rivets, which were deliberately rivetted slightly 'proud' of the skin, would have to be flush-milled. A lot of flush-milling would be kneeling down on one's knees. This was how I got housemaid's knee. True! I was set up for an operation on my knee, but when the contract ended a year later, the swelling around my knees cleared up and I was discharged from hospital, because at that particular time I was in no pain.

John said that one day, when he retired, he would sell his house, buy a horsebox or large furniture lorry, kit it out with bunk beds (like a caravan really) with one exception. He would buy a Harley-Davidson motorcycle, put it inside the caravan too and travel the world touring, and wherever they stopped he would get out the Harley, and with his wife riding pillion, would bomb around the countryside at leisure.

Do you know, John Gaudian did just that! It was a pleasure to know him and his wife. I shall never forget you John, your sense of humour and your very presence would just light up the room. Goodbye old friend, 'til we meet again'. Diamond Geezer, that's what you were.

One of the most interesting jobs but, though I say it myself, the most skilled, was the installation of the flying controls. Now, though I viewed this job and admired the person fitting the pulleys, quadrants, pulley wires, split-pinning the castellated nuts, etc, I thought never in a creation of cats do I *ever* want to do *that* job.

What happened? The operator doing the job applied for and got an inspection job, and who was asked to replace him? Me! I tell you, it was with a certain amount of fear and trepidation that I took on the job of doing the flying controls and, once I'd cracked it and sussed out how it was best accomplished, it was found to be very enjoyable and rewarding to do. I grew to love that job in the end. How strange.

Back on the home front, as regards my Christian walk with the Lord, I was attending Ryde Elim Church. Pastor Neil Broomhead and his wife Ruth came to Albert Street in Ryde and Neil asked me to become a Deacon and become part of the 'Deaconate' in the Elim Church. Spiritually, I was still only a 'baby Christian' in many ways. I had much to learn but we all have to start somewhere, don't we?

One job I was asked to do was sharing the job of 'Youth Leader' with Bernard Parkman, when a solicitor by the name of Mr Percy Rolfe donated what was known as the 'Binstead Hut', just off Jellicoe Road in Binstead, to the church. Pastor Neil Broomhead would also officiate too, as the oversight.

Bernard also was a Deacon and trained to become a minister. He had his own following, eventually starting his own little church with its members comprising an evangelical Apostolic church.

The number coming to the estate varied from week to week. One week there could be thirty youngsters and the following week barely half a dozen. The ages ranged from five years to fifteen years, so we had to split them up into appropriate age groups. One week, one of the eight-year olds started playing up, so we told him to leave and banned him for the next two weeks. Two minutes later, armed with a piece of 3" x 2" timber three feet long, he started to stove in the door. This was when the Reverend Neil Broomhead nearly lost his sanctification (livelihood). He chased after the lad and inwardly I was screaming for the little so-and-so to get away. I don't know what Neil would have done, but I knew he was pretty wound up and it was as well he didn't catch him.

Do you know what the rest of the kids wanted to do? They wanted to ban him altogether. I mean, that young lad could be such a disruptive influence, he really could. Anyway, we sent him packing for the obligatory two weeks and that was that.

On one night after the youth club had finished, about ten minutes before actually, it began to rain.

Bernard said to me, "John, can you do the honours and lock up the Binstead Hut? I'll be on my way, and I'll take some of the kids home who've further to go."

"Okay," says I. "We'll see each other in church on Sunday, yeah?"

Anyway, by the time I'd outed the lights, locked up the premises and gone to my car, the heavens opened up. The rain was coming down like stair-rods. Now I have to journey to East Cowes, where I lived in Clarence Road. Unfortunately I needed to go to the loo – I was breaking my neck, so to speak. Passing through Wootton High Street, no other car in sight, by now the rain was sheeting it down and I needed to get home and sort myself out, if you get my drift.

Passing the Sloop Inn at Wootton, I noticed a car parked up, no lights, but with the engine running. I'm doing approximately 36-37 miles an hour, when the car's headlights came on and followed me. I had, shall we say, misgivings that all was not well.

He was too close to me to see if he had the statutory blue light on the roof, and it wasn't until I got to the top of the rise by Harwoods Garage, that my worst fears had been confirmed. Yeah, it was Mr Plod, and he was hard up my rear, ready to pounce. From Harwoods Garage, I believe I could have been credited with 'Driver of the Year' as I conformed exactly to the norm and drove within the speed limit. At Whippingham, the flashing blue lights, plus much flashing of the headlights, indicated for me to pull over.

"Will you wind your window down sir?"

"Yes constable, what's the problem?"

"Well sir, you do realise you were speeding up Wootton High Street don't you sir?"

"Was I constable? I'm sorry to hear that, how fast was I going then?"

"39 miles an hour sir. Have you got your driving licence or documents with you sir?"

"No constable," I replied, "I don't carry them in the car in case they get nicked!"

"I see sir, I'll need to take down your details and, by the way, will you bring your documents into Newport Police Station within the next three days?"

"I certainly will constable. By the way, do you enjoy your job? I mean, it's tipping it down with rain, there's no other traffic on the road and you've got your engine running, without the lights on, to snare some poor so-and-so like a rabbit caught in a trap? In other words, you ambush them!"

"Just doing my job sir. If people kept to the speed limit there wouldn't be a problem sir, would there?"

"Just out of interest constable, do you carve another notch on your truncheon each time you catch some poor sap like me?"

"Just doing my job sir. Incidentally, if you have any more questions, I must warn you and remind you, that anything you say.."

I then interrupted him and said, "Just book me constable and have done with it and I'll try and be a good boy from now on, alright?"

"I think that concludes the matter, goodnight sir."

"Goodnight to you constable – and thank you for your attention to duty today sir."

"Thank you, sir, goodnight." He just had to have the last word, didn't he?"

Two weeks later, I was fined £28 quid for my sins.

Anyway, back to the Binstead Hut and my youth Club work. To do the job of a youth leader, because Bernard and I had done training courses with our work in the Sunday School, youth work and all it entails was like an extension of the Sunday School.

I was very aware there are strict guidelines concerning the training and care of young children, and also, that if we show them respect, they will normally settle down and be receptive to what we adults do, in order to command their respect.

This was illustrated when things went slightly awry, when a visiting children's evangelist from Newcastle took matters into his own hands when one young boy wouldn't stop talking and was, frankly, messing things up for the other children.

The evangelist marched up to the back of the hut, told the young boy, an 11 year old, to stand up, then taking hold of him by the ear, propelled him down to the front of the other children and sat him on the seat.

Now this evangelist was here on the Island for a weeklong children's crusade, and was staying with Bernard and his wife Audrie, for the duration. Now we finished each day at around 4pm. At about 5.30pm there was a knock, knock at the door, and when Bernard went to answer it, was confronted by an irate parent with her husband in tow.

She wished to speak to the evangelist who had made her son into a laughing-stock, and beside that, taking hold of a young person by the ear was not only dangerous for the young lad but could be construed as criminal assault. (Technically she was spot on, even though, in reality, it was a storm in a teacup).

The boy's father didn't say a dicky-bird, he just nodded sheepishly in support. The evangelist did come to the door, whereby he was berated by the mum and had to eat humble pie, acknowledge his short-comings and apologise profusely in order to diffuse the situation.

At the end of the day, honour had been upheld and Mum and Dad went away with a job well done. Or was it? You see, I was inside Bernard's house looking out across the road, and what was the lad in question doing? He was grinning from ear to ear (no pun intended) and laughing his socks off at the discomfort of the evangelist when his mum was remonstrating with him. No, the boy's pride was hurt, no more than that, and his mum failed to see that had her son been well behaved the incident would not have happened. The mother had done her son no favours whatsoever, even though she was right.

Now I'd like to extol the attributes of a certain riveter who I had the privilege to know. He's gone to glory now, but he was certainly a character. He was extrovert and was larger than life really.

Very few people knew Ken who, originally with his brother Alfie, were living in Marks Corner (or close by). Marks Corner, should you go down Pallance Road, Northwood, on reaching the bottom of the road, bear left, head towards Porchfield and on the way you will come to Marks Corner.

How do I know so much about Ken? When I worked in J.S. White's, his brother Alfie ran the drawing store, just inside on the left, at fitters-on-board department. Alfie's job, believe it or not, was to keep an old iron stove burning (it had a metal chimney leading up to the lower part of the roof). This was to protect the drawing store from getting too damp and kept the drawings in pristine condition.

We fitters, on our lunchbreaks, would often congregate, especially in winter, at the store and warm ourselves up a bit before going out on board ship, which was as cold as charity until fitted out.

Here then is what Alfie had to say about his brother Ken.

"Our Ken was awarded the 'Burma Star', a military medal, for fighting with the Chindits in the jungles of Burma. When he came home after the war, his nerves were shot to pieces."

Why, you may ask, was he wounded at all?

"No," replies Alfie, "but fighting an invisible enemy and having alongside each Tommy Atkins, would be a Gurkha, one of the silent assassins that the Japanese, of all their enemies, feared most of all."

Our Ken's nerves were on a knife-edge each and every day of that campaign whilst in Burma. From time to time, the Gurkha assigned to their British counterpart would make a foray into the jungle, doing what only Gurkhas do best, which is to locate the whereabouts of their enemy. If the Gurkha came across one of the enemy, he would be 'dispatched' by the Gurkha, for want of a better word, and the left ear of the Japanese soldier severed and brought back as proof of a 'kill'. This ensured the Gurkha concerned would receive a small payment for accomplishing the deed.

This was alright, but at those times the British Tommy was on his own without his Gurkha companion. "After not just weeks or months but for years, once the trauma of war was over, the brain had to somehow recover from the stress of permanently being keyed-up, pressure, pressure, pressure, all the time. It was simply relentless and when Ken came home, he wasn't the same old Ken that I, as his brother, knew before he was enlisted into the army – he'd suffered a nervous breakdown."

"Running alongside the lane where we used to live, was a two to three-acre field. Our Ken used to go out in that field, and for day after day, just walk and walk and walk round it."

"Alf", says my mother, "go and get your brother indoors, that can't be doing him any good, walking around a field, day after day."

Then Dad interrupted his wife, and said, "You leave our Ken alone, he's dealing with the situation in his own way."

"He'll come out of it in time, don't interfere lass, he'll get over it, he just needs to be left alone for now, just leave 'im be, don't interfere."

Three to four months later, Ken started to come out his shell. It was as though he'd shut down his mind and body to everything around him. It was a defence mechanism that cocooned him from the worries of the world.

I finally managed to track down Ken's wife, Valerie, and their offspring Graham and Sarah, now living in Wootton. Val and I, with Ken when he was alive, go back a long way. Valerie and Ken lived in a small two up, two down cottage in the bend of the road at Niton. Val used to keep that little cottage immaculate. It was a joy to visit our Ken and Val as they were always welcoming to Marian and I.

At that time, approximately in 1965 (the year before our solitary World Cup win in 1966, this is why I can remember the year of our first meeting) my wife and I lived in Shorwell, by the way.

The reason I went to see Ken at his home was to work on his 'Moggie Minor'. Although Ken would try to keep the car on the road and to keep the engine going somehow, it was, to put it another way, rather sluggish and needed attention.

I'm an aircraft fitter, although time served as an apprentice at J.S. White's qualified me to be accepted at Saunders Roe at that time, due to a redundancy situation at White's. I would repair car engines from time to time, removing the head from the engine and regrinding the valves etc. Checking out the spark plugs and the distributor cap, always replacing the head gasket as a matter of course. The engine sounded as though it was 'knackered', for want of a better word, but when I'd stripped it down, it was in pristine condition.

"Ken, there's nothing wrong with this engine mate, so what's going on?"

"Ah," says Ken. "I forgot to tell you, somebody has already worked on it and it's worse than it was before I got it looked at the first time, which is why I sent for you."

"Cheers mate," says I. "Let's get it sorted. Let's check the oil level Ken, shall we?"

"No problem," says Ken. "I replaced the oil myself."

"Oh, did you now," says I. "Let's check it anyway."

The oil level was approximately *three inches* above the top markings on the dip stick.

"Ken, did you check the oil levels?"

"No need to," says Ken. "I filled it up myself 'til I could get no more oil in, that's alright isn't it?"

I gave a big sigh of relief.

"No, it isn't alright but I've found out the problem."

Ken had overfilled it.

"Ken, get your drip-tray, we've got to empty out some of that oil. The oil marks on your dip-stick are there for a reason. You should *not* run your engine if the oil mark shows the level *below* minimum, and it also goes for the level *above* the top level on the old dip-stick."

We drained the required amount and obviously the engine then ran as sweet as a nut.

"Bootsie Boy's fixed the car Val," says Ken.

"No, I haven't," says I. "You fixed it up good and proper Ken when you overfilled it. Don't let it happen ever again, alright?"

Ken was over the moon.

"Bl***dy 'ell Boots, what do I owe yer?"

I said, "On yer way mate, have one on me, Ken-boy." 'Nuff said!

Now to Ken's Army career. Ken was born in 1933 and died in 2018 making him 85 years old. He was one of nine children, most of them boys. He lived in a tiny two-up, two-down cottage near Marks Corner, as I've said before. Ken and his brothers were always fighting.

Ken joined the Pioneer Corps, then when his 'call-up' papers arrived, enlisted in the Royal Electrical Mechanical Engineers and for a time and a season was an official driver.

Ken did training with the 6th Airborne Division, Parachute Regiment, attached to the R.E.M.E. He qualified for his 'wings', which is the cap-badge awarded to the successful trainees who were able to complete the course.

I've held that cap-badge in the palm of my hand and looked at the wings and the parachute, the one with a round canopy in the act of descendancy, so I know *that's* true, dear reader. If anyone wants to dispute this, I'll see you outside, we'll take it from there.

Ken was sent to Burma, and after the Burma campaign served with his regiment in Korea. After the Korean saga had fizzled out, our Ken was then sent to Malaya, where he finished his army career – virtually a broken man but, with his family around him, the trauma of warfare, at the sharp end no less, was now behind him. Time, they say, is a great healer.

It *did* take time, but happy-go-lucky Ken did come through. Another thing that Valerie told me, Ken was a good amateur boxer in the British Army and he was as hard as nails. Whilst working at BHC (Saunders Roe had changed its name) Ken was in the toilets of Columbine. Two other so-called work colleagues were discussing Ken not knowing that Ken was in one of the cubicles. Ken emerges from the toilet, and button-holed these two herberts and speaks to them, especially the one shooting his mouth of.

"Look here pal, if you've got anything to say about me, have the guts to say it to my face will you?"

With that, Ken pulls back his fist, and punches the idiot in the mouth.

He then says these words in parting, "Have you got the message?"

Ken never did pull his punches.

In the words of Michael Caine, the actor, "not a lot of people know that" (but I did). And very few people knew what that happy-go-lucky, larger than life character had gone through during the war, especially at GKN – but I did!

It was another privileged person I'd got to work with over the years. I salute you Ken boy, it was lovely to work alongside you!

# Chapter 8

*This and That – Incidents along Life's Way*

I didn't always work on aircraft and hovercraft, which I will share with you, and it concerns a project that was made at Siemens, Plessey in Cowes.

This job was the XR3D Radar Cabin and without giving away any military secrets, had a wave-guide that enabled the trained operator to 'see' over the horizon. There was a pay dispute at Cowes, where it was being manufactured, and an unofficial go-slow was hampering its progress. Plessey, in their infinite wisdom, 'farmed' it out to GKN, for want of a better word, to advance the project. Apart from preliminary work on the walls of the cabin, the job was going nowhere in a hurry. You see, although 80% of the details to build it were forthcoming, a very shrewd knowledgeable work-force over at Cowes had deliberately left out the two main pieces of equipment at the beginning or start off point, or the end of the system to build. To put it bluntly, the job was really going nowhere.

Yours truly, moi, had even been given a slight wage rise by being elevated in status to 'leading hand'. This was much to the annoyance of John Achison, our shop-steward (a good one at that), because me, a lowly fitter, was now earning, for a short time and a season, more than him. He was not a happy bunny, I can tell you.

It was during this project that Bert Spall, my works manager at Falcon Yard, urged me, when the dispute was over, and the parts forthcoming, to by-pass the copper-smiths and fit the copper pipes myself.

"Well, you've fitted pipework before Bootsie, haven't you? I mean to say, you were doing it all the time at Sammy White's, yeah?"

"Well, yes Bert," I replied, "but the coppersmiths union'll go bananas if they find out, won't it?"

"Go on Bootsie, I'll not say anything. Besides, if it advances the job it'll be worth it."

"On your head be it Bert as you are the boss. I'll do it but I'm not taking the blame if the unions dig their heels in, okay?"

Within two hours, a lone coppersmith reported back to the coppersmith steward based at Old Road, on the north site. From there, the steward contacted the works convenor, Vic Williams. Then the fat hit the fan, as there was now the potential for strike action (with me caught in the middle). The convenor (our own from A.E.U.) gave me a lecture. Protestations of innocence cut no ice with not just *our* union but everybody really. To me, it was another storm in a teacup. And Bert? He just left me high and dry.

His take on the situation? "Well, I did have slight misgivings about what John was doing maybe."

'Misgivings' – he jolly well told me, in not so many words, to do it but I think induced amnesia caused him to forget that.

When it was all over, and I'd been given a 'rocket' by the Unions, that old rascal, my works manager Bert, said "Yeah, but Bootsie, we (the proverbial we) did advance the job somewhat, didn't we? I mean, we're definitely further ahead because of it, aren't we?"

Another interesting job I worked on, but only in a very small way, was the Black Night rocket project. In Falcon Yard, in one corner of the hangar, was a large wire cage and it was built especially for security reasons to house the nose-cone of the rocket.

Now, how is it, you may ask, can you come up with all these facts and be accurate as regards the subject matter? I'm one of those people who have a very good memory going right back to when I was about three years old. I'm good at remembering names and faces, as well as incidents that happened and why. If I had an axe to grind, I could certainly drop a lot of people in it, knowing what, and who, I know, but that's not my way. By knowing what job I was working on at the time, I could even pinpoint with some degree of accuracy what year and time.

That's not my style. *People*, that's what I'm about. I like to study people, what makes them tick, why are they so irascible, angry, all the time. There is always an underlying reason as to why certain people are the way they are, and my leanings towards Christianity (due in the main to a praying wife for initially my salvation) have certainly done me in good stead.

I no longer have the same degree of anger inside me that I used to feel as a young man. Although I'm ashamed to admit it, as a contractor, I struck out at two men who wouldn't back off when I was a contractor in West Germany. The first idiot wouldn't let me pass by him in the corridor at the hostel where we were staying. Well, I never fight fair, never had done. I learnt that from my childhood days. England and Scotland were playing an International at the end of this particular week, and this Scotsman said, "Aye, ye sassanack, ye, we'll beat ye on Saturday so we will."

"Let me pass Jock, I need to go to work," I said.

"Make me!" says Jock.

"You won't like it when I do", says I.

At that, with his foot raised, he ran at me. I thought, here we go. I was carrying a small raincoat and quick as a flash, I threw it over his face. He couldn't see a thing, then I punched him in the stomach as hard as I could and dropped him. Retrieving my coat, I hissed at him, "You try that lark on me again, and I'll really get mad with you. Have a good day, and I'd advise you to get some kip in." Chè sera sera.

I happened to put another guy, Kevin Delaney, off work for three weeks, who had, unbeknown to me, a duodenal ulcer. He was from Hull. He was very good at 'touch Karate' and for six or seven minutes with me as his guinea pig, he was showing off to his mates. They were all laughing at his antics, especially when he would sweep his foot past my ear, just brushing it with the side of it. He wasn't hurting me, but my *pride* was hurt. The contractors started laughing, then the *Germans* started chortling away. That's it, enough is enough (says I to myself). Because the moves he was doing were repetitive, I knew what to do. With controlled anger, I just exploded into action and karate punched him in the gut. He fell like a stone, job done!

I'll not be going on about my prowess as a fighting man, because, as a Christian, it doesn't say much for the 'turn the other cheek' way of doing things. This third and last incident, nearly got me court-martialed when I was twenty years old, in the Territorial Army. One young man from Manchester had only recently joined and for some reason or another just kept taking the mickey out of me. The other lads started saying, "You're not going to stand for that Bootsie, are you?"

I sighed. I suppose I'd better do something. Well, we were on manoeuvres, and with thunder flashes going and in arrow-formation with a Bren gunner on each flank, we marched down this field.

At the bottom of the field, I caught up with the young bloke from Manchester, and decided to sort him out. Unfortunately, Barry from West Cowes, kept trying to come between us and to diffuse the situation (blessed are the peacemakers, comes to mind), but I was having none of it.

"If you interfere once more Barry, I'll down yer," I says to Barry.

"Don't do it, Bootsie." says Barry, it's not worth it. Barry steps in again, don't say I didn't warn you Barry, and with the bolt hatching .303 Lee Enfield rifle I was carrying, I stoved it into his stomach and poor old Barry fell where he once stood. Right at that very moment the regular soldier, a Bombardier no less, caught me in the act. He'd been watching our progress all the time and was not amused.

"Right Private, your Army number?"

"23 88 38 54 Sir," I shouts out.

"Well Private, what have we here? Let me inform you sunshine, you might think that this two weeks Army Camp is just a stroll in the park and you then go home.

"Not so, Private. Should I put you on a charge, and what I've just witnessed believe you me I could, you'd be heading for the glasshouse. It's not impossible for even a part-time soldier like yourself to be court-martialed. Do I make myself clear, Private?"

"Loud and clear, Sir. Loud and clear." I replied.

By the time the army exercise was over, it was back to the Drill Hall. My simmering resentment on how the day had panned out once again exploded into my loss of temper  Unfortunately, because of the violence in my life as a child, being brought up to view it at first hand from the age of five, I grew to actually love fighting. It was an adrenalin rush to the head.

Then I spotted my Mancunian friend, got him in a head lock, started with a half-Nelson, finished with a full Nelson, and with an arm barred across his windpipe, lowered him to the ground.  I'd cut off his air supply somewhat, then wrapped my legs around his stomach in a body scissors, I locked my legs together until he literally screamed for mercy. I'm afraid I used to be a bit of an animal in those days.  I was in no mood, after being threatened with being court - martialed because of this edjit.

The other lads told me to let him go and with great reluctance I did so, but he got the message, didn't he?

After coming back from West Germany nearly two years after starting off in 1973, as I said before, by saving hard and not wasting money, the deposit we owed to John A. was paid off in full, all £900 of it, leaving just the premium to pay, that and of course the interest. We had at last a terrace house, indeed an _end_ of terrace house, technically making it into a semi-detached terrace house. We were on the bottom rung of the ladder though.  I worked under Lofty Argyles, as I wrote earlier on, but aircraft fitting was what I really wanted to do. I asked Lofty if I could be transferred down to the airframe section of Falcon Yard, as I wanted to do the job I was trained to do.  If you want to go, said Lofty, I'd rather you went than stay and become resentful.  Lofty arranged the transfer and I went with his blessing.

I was now working on the Lynx contract, a helicopter being built for the RAF. It was in that department that I worked on the Black Arrow.  One interesting snippet of information comes to mind, it is simply this:

Paint shop, especially Jock Taylor, had the enviable task of the spraying of the Black Arrow nose cones, which constitutes the main reason for the rocket's existence, because the recovery of the nose cone _intact_ is the key to its success.

Jock had to spray a rubbery type of solution onto the nose cone, not *once,* but *20 times*. Each spray coat was added in 60 second intervals. This equates to 20 minutes plus spraying time, about 40 minutes in all. "Did it work?" you may ask. Yes, it certainly did. I can vouch for that because a nose cone that had been orbiting the earth, suffers the most incredible heat on the face taking the full force of the re-entry, when the cone glows red-hot with the heat that the re-entry generates. When the blackened and charred protective covering that Jock Taylor had previously sprayed on before the launch was peeled off, the nose cone itself was completely intact. The secret formula of that rubbery type layer of protection had done its job.

I believe the formula for producing this special spray was developed at GKN – 'nuff said.

Not all the work I did was on aircraft, hovercraft or landing craft, because of waiting time, which entailed waiting around until given a job. One such job was laying 18" x 18" carpet tiles. We fitters had to prepare the floor, sweeping, hoovering up and with a very long-handled paintbrush, coating the floor with a tile adhesive – with a difference. Although the tiles were well and truly stuck to the floor, the adhesive never went off. The tiles could be lifted, even years later. The function of the tile adhesive was just to keep the tiles in place, *not* to permanently glue them in a way that would damage them.

Another interesting job was cutting and fitting ceiling tiles. Some fitters belly-ached about doing certain jobs, but hey, the powers-that-be paid me my wages. I mean, I'd sweep the floor as long as they paid me a skilled man's wage. It's no skin off my nose, as they say.

Now I'd like to talk about a subject that's close to my heart. Music, country music as much as anything else, and singing coupled with my walk with the Lord of Lords and King of Kings – Jeshua (or Jesus Christ).

As a young lad of 9, 10 or 11 years of age, I was always singing the pop songs of a different era – the 1940s, 50s and 60s. I would go to bed at Cuthbert Road, Portsmouth and I'd hunker down below the bedclothes, secreting the little radio, tuned into Radio Luxembourg for the top 20 songs of the day in the charts.

My maternal grandmother was Irish, and although she died before I was born, I inherited her collection of Irish country music. (Bridie Gallagher and others spring to mind.) When I grew up, I went to Sunday School. I nearly joined the Church Choir, at St Mary's, Fratton, Portsmouth. Anyway, later on in life, when I returned to the Island after 1975, when my time in West Germany was over, my prowess with the guitar started to improve.

Although I was limited without a knowledge of music in general, it was by hearing and listening for the chord changes. I instinctively knew when to ask someone for advice, and rightly or wrongly, *knew* when to add another minor chord, to the three chord wonders I was already playing.

Eventually, Pastor Neil's wife, Ruth, asked me if I would accompany her by playing my guitar and also singing, which I was pleased to do. Ruth had a cracking soprano voice and I would accompany her by singing harmony, by singing the descant.

It was a joy to sing with the Pastor's wife and we seemed to gel together as a singing duo. We would sing the cover songs of Pastor Len Meghee, who wrote and sang country songs. Also, songs by Mary Mckee and the Genesis too, were added to our repertoire of song Ministry (they were an Irish group).

Now for a true story – an answer to prayer. One evening, when Marian and I were still living in East Cowes, Reverend Tony Anderson paid us a social visit, seeing as he had just taken a visitor to the Red Funnel ferry. The visitor was a foot passenger on the ferry, and would come to the Island, to our meetings, from Southampton.

When we were all having a cup of tea and bickies at Clarence Road where I lived, the subject of music, naturally, cropped up.

"Tony, in my head, I've composed no end of songs, but I just cannot get my head around writing the lyrics."

"Let's pray", said Tony, "Let the Lord give you the skills to write songs". Later, God answered that prayer.

Tony prayed (this would be about 9pm in the evening). Tony then departed and, after we said our goodbyes, I then decided to start getting ready for bed. Marian and I would normally hit the hay at around 1030pm as I would normally get up around 6.45am in the morning.

I honestly had forgotten the prayer request to Tony, about composing lyrics for Gospel songs, when, at approximately 11pm and not even thinking about Gospel songs, the words to my very first Gospel song were just buzzing in my brain. I quickly got out of bed, and 20 minutes (*yes, 20 minutes later*) the song was written.

The words:
*Is it time friend, is it time, that you broke, the chains that bind?*
*The links that tie you to the world, its glitter, greed and sin unfurled.*
*The sin that soils, a troubled life, from drink to drugs and untold strife.*

(Chorus)
*Won't you come, the way of the cross, the world, its toys, they're no*
*great loss, yield your heart to Christ this day,*
*He only can your fears allay.*

There *are* more verses but that is my first song. My wife and two daughters, Caroline and Kathleen, in their teens, combined with myself to make a foursome, forming a different singing group.

But, the icing on the proverbial cake, was singing with the Reverend Tony Anderson (brother to Jon Anderson of Jon & Vangelis and 'Chariots of Fire' fame). Tony and his brother Jon came from Manchester and they, with two others, formed a band before Tony was to split up with the group (he was married, the others were not so there was a parting of the ways).

Tony himself was a bit of a headliner in the island of Majorca. In tragic circumstances, when his wife died (Tony's testimony to tell), Tony returned to the Island and lived in Reed Street, Oakfield, Ryde.

I led the singing as a worship leader in the Albert Street, Elim Church for a time and a period, but when Tony Anderson came on the scene I gradually opted out of leading because Tony was a more 'gifted' musician. Tony used to ask me to join him in taking a service at H.M.P. Camp Hill. As a songwriter now myself, it was *my* songs that Tony insisted we play, even though Tony was a more prolific writer and eventually formed a Christian group called 'Chasidim', a Greek word meaning kind, pious.

(Psalm 18:26) with the kind thus showest thyself kind. K.T.V. Chasidim means: with Salutation, let thy saints rejoice!

Another Greek word that I've grown very familiar with, for over thirty years, is 'SOZO' which means saved, healed, made whole in Jesus – SOZO.

Now dear readers, please, please bear with me, just for the next few pages, as regards my spiritual side. It is this side of my character that makes me tick. So, forbear, if you will.

I'm Church of England (C. of E.) and was christened with the name of John Brian Bettenson, after both John (after King John) and Brian (after Irish King Brian Boru) who achieved the distinction of becoming High King of Ireland. He first became King of Munster, then subjugated Leinster to achieve this. Just a little bit of Irish history – through my maternal grandmother's Irish roots.

Sozo Ministries International was established in 1983 by Pastor Marion Daniel. Now another Marian (my wife – her name spelt slightly differently) used to go to the Elim Conference at Bognor Regis, once a year, at Butlins Holiday Camp, out of season, when it was cheaper.

It was there my youngest daughter, Alison, became friendly with Kim, another girl of the same age. By the time the Conference was ended, the girl's mother Jackie had exchanged addresses with me and my family and offered to pick up me and my family at Southampton car park by the ferry terminal.

Originally, we would go to Mountbatten School, off the Botley Road, in the school's gymnasium. Sozo Ministries is *not* a church by the way. It is a Christian organisation whereby people with their problems, whether of a spiritual nature or not, can be ministered to.

Christine and Rhonda are both very gifted and understanding Christian women, who designate which members of the Sozo team should be best suited to the needs of each individual of the general public.

Rhonda (bless her) doesn't pull her punches but says it as it is, always backed up by God's Word and with feeling.

Christine, on the other hand (also, I might add, a gifted keyboard player and worship leader) is very, very, adept at 'pairing up' the best person to meet the needs of the visitor who needs help.

Normally, there will be two people meeting a person's needs, and let me tell you this, I'm not ashamed to confess tears of pure joy on my part during prayer ministry sessions. Thank you, Richard C.

It isn't just about talking through a person's problems. The Ministry Team try to get to the root of the problem and deal with it, root and branch, as the saying goes.

Sozo are now ensconced at Dunwood Oaks, Awbridge, just outside of Romsey, along Danes Road. If there is anything you wish to discuss with the prayer team over the telephone, then please do so, they really are brilliant at their jobs and are anointed to help you.

I offer my thanks to Paul and Kate, Richard and Helen, Nigel, Liz, Roz, Sue, Arthur and Sue, and please, if I've not mentioned you by name, especially Simon and his lovely Irish wife Rachel, then please forgive me.

Special thanks are forthcoming to Joan Daniel (Pastor Marion's Mum) and Valerie.

Alan, one of Marian's brothers, last but not least, a special thank you. I salute you too, Bro.

These, dear readers, are some of the body of people who have helped Marian and I on our spiritual journey through the pathway of life.

Both my wife and I have Jewish roots. Me on my maternal grandmother's side and Marian, on the other hand, also Jewish roots from her maternal grandmother but that's her testimony, not mine.

Now many of you reading this book will undoubtedly know of the incident that marks me out as one of the biggest clowns in industrial history – *that* incident. That could only happen to be one of the bestest aeronautical incidents, as all of you will know of this calamitous, catastrophic claptrap. (Note the use of alliteration there that only a born writer such as I could have written) – now read on.

Nick T. (the big fat git, his words not mine), reminded me when I bumped into him in Hursts recently. I say 'bumped' into him, because he is now of such a size that for several seconds the sun's rays were blotted out and darkness caused people to stumble around!

Anyway, the mallet incident. Oh, and here I also owe my son Kieron, who met up with his sister Caroline near Rylstone Gardens in Shanklin, a brief mention, as that same incident was brought up in conversation and the two of them were almost rolling about with laughter because of it. Thanks a bunch, Kieron old son.

Here goes then. I was on nights and was working on the north site of Columbine department, the Union Flag Hanger. Another so-called fitter and I had to move an overhead crane that although was the answer to the problem of lifting an extremely heavy component, unfortunately was not readily available – we had to move the damn thing.

"Permission to speak," says the prat of a fitter assisting me on that fateful night.

"Go on," says I, wearily.

"I've got a good idea, how we can move the crane," says he.

"Let's do it then." says I.

The crane was moved by hand, by chains.

"Well, if we gets a very long piece of string," says he, "we can tie a wooden mallet to the string and tie it to the chain."

I then interjected with, "Yeah, a tightly tied clove hitch." (A knot like what I learned to do in East Cowes Boys Brigade.) "A tightly tied clove hitch, with a piece of binder twine from the local farming community should suffice," I sarcastically said.

"No, no, no," says my oppo, "I've got just the thing to do it with, here, whaddya think Boots?"

"Should work, yeah, let's go for it, let's get this problem sorted," says I.

So we did. We succeeded, but when the flying mallet incident finally happened, I was stood on one of the jigs to catch the soddin' mallet, by the way, after butthead had tossed the thing high over the girder. Well, it swung like a pendulum, heading straight for me, in a parabolic curve, so damn fast, and, because of where I was stood, I had nowhere to go.

*Smack!* The heavy part of the mallet struck me in the mouth with such force it split my upper denture, with me ending up with a mouthful of blood.

Hurt? You bet your sweet life it hurt. With hindsight, I should have retired hurt and clocked out and gone home, but I didn't. Stoically, I soldiered on, to the amusement of many of my colleagues which has immortalised me in the annals of fame, as one of the real characters who ever worked in Saunders Roe, now GKN. Cheers Nick, cheers Kieron, for reminding me. How thoughtful of you both. In my own words, dear reader, that, unfortunately, is something that will forever be remembered in GKN's hall of fame by all and sundry.

"Sein oder nicht sein, das ist di frage!" "To be or not to be, that is the question?"

I will now list a whole bunch of incidents which caused my eldest daughter Caroline and Kieron such amusement. Here goes – not necessarily in chronological order.

The apple-pie bed incident. This involved my brother-in-law Joe, the one who emigrated to Australia with his wife to be, Linda, just over 50 years ago and still counting. This involved an Aerial Square 4 motorcycle, a tow rope and a clapped-out old Norton 19s motorcycle, 600cc. I used to live in Shorwell at the time and any telephone calls came from our next-door neighbour. David, the Wood's son, came to tell us that Joe, Marian's brother, was marooned in Yarmouth where he was working to supplement his money from the bank, by working part time as a Kitchen Porter.

On the night in question, at about 9.30pm, I was asked to take a towing rope to haul him and his Aerial Square 4 back to Shorwell. When I arrived at the chalets, Joe had already stripped the engine down, to try and get it going. He failed, because the head gasket, I believe, was 'shot', so it was a big no-no. Finally, I arrived.

"What's the game plan mate?" says I, bearing in mind it was now 1015pm.

"Well, I know it don't look too good John, but I do have a spare head gasket. I'm pretty sure that we can get this thing going."

So, with oil and petrol permeating the chalet that Joe was allocated, Joe sets to work. An hour later, he's tightening up the last of the nuts, that had to be torqued up for the 4 piper to be fired up.

"Come on then Joe, get it started then" says I. Zilch, nothing doing.

By this time, it was now nearly 1145pm. In the event, I had to tow him anyway. But first the chalet had to be tidied up. This took nearly half an hour, and the dirt and oil and muck had to be cleaned off the floor. Joe ripped the bedsheet in half. One half became rags to mop up the detritus in Joe's chalet. The other half of the sheet became an apple-pie bed, whereby the sheet was folded in half and presented, for all the world to see, as a properly made up bed, with two sheets, when in reality it wasn't.

The old enemy of time had moved on to 1215 and some. We sets off, with my old workhorse, the Norton, towing the Aerial, at a quarter to one (1245). We carried on over the Yarmouth bridge, and then carried along to Betty Haunt Lane which exits onto the main Calbourne to Carisbrooke road.

Just as I was beginning to emerge from Betty Haunt Lane, we see a jam-jar (Police car) coming from the opposite direction. The driver looked straight at us, and I said to Joe, who was being towed on the Aerial Square 4, "What shall we do now mate?"

"We carry on going, as quickly as possible. We can just about make it to Nodgham Lane, and as soon as we get round the bend at Nodgham Lane we'll switch off the engine."

We heard the sound of the Police car go past Nodgham Lane, bearing in mind we were hidden from view, with my engine turned off, and then we set off again. Finally, we arrived at Shorwell, where I lived.

"Joe, if we tippy-toe indoors, I really think Marian will be asleep. You go and kip on the sofa, and I'll try and go upstairs without disturbing her."

Fat chance! I opened the front door to be greeted by Marian. She was not a happy bunny. We didn't own mobile phones, they were expensive in those days.

"What sort of time do you think this is then John?"

"No idea", says I, "but it must be late." Marian's comments I'm afraid are unprintable. C'est la vie. She blotted her copy-book good and proper I might tell you that night.

Joe and I go back to 1961, so Joe would have been about 14 years old. I taught the little perisher how to play chess. A year later, he was starting to beat me. As he grew older, we grew closer. At the age of 18 years, after a final altercation and breakdown of relationships, I exited the Cemetery Lodge where I lived and left home, pushing a second-hand bike that Grandad had made, and a few worldly possessions. I was free! I had nowhere to go, so went to my girlfriend's house in Long Lane and asked if I could just stay the night.

Marian's mum said, if you like, and you pay your way, you can stay longer if you wish. The rest is history and I would ride that old 3 speed pushbike to Cowes, where I worked at J.S.White's shipyard, parking the bike in the bike-shed at Thetis Road gate.

When Joe got older, and could legally own a motorcycle, he bought a "Sunbeam S7" motorcycle with 'balloon' tyres. A shaft driven bike, which he loved. He could do anything on that bike, even kneeling on the darned thing whilst steering it with his hands, copying the showing-off streak he'd copied off me. (No, he was a good rider, even at that young age of 17).

Eventually, as Joe started courting a very attractive young lady from Newchurch, by the name of Linda, they all emigrated to Adelaide, which is in South Australia.

My wife Marian and I have visited Australia four times, usually having to land in Sydney and travelling by coach (Greyhound) or even train to get to Adelaide. The city of Adelaide now has its own International Airport, so we travel direct, usually, after a stopover in Singapore, to Adelaide, where Joe and Linda would greet us, and ferry us back to their 'single-storey' house. Just a fancy description for a 'bungalow', Aussie style.

They've now been there 50 years or more and are fully integrated to the Aussie lifestyle. Joe has enjoyed taking on 'franchises' for Bridgestone, the tyre people, and has owned 'garages' geared up to do wheel bearings and anything mechanical that a car requires, to keep it safe on the road.

Joe has found his 'niche' in life and has done well. He had a beautiful daughter Lisa, and a son called Jason, who works for the 'Continental' tyre company. Jason has done exceptionally well.

Sadly, Lisa only lived until her 25th birthday, and the love that Joe and Linda had, and still have, in their hearts for that young lady Lisa, is something to behold. The illness and round the clock care became a routine of such proportions that Joe and Linda had to share the night-time duties that entailed moving her and preventing Lisa from having bed-sores. Lisa's illness was predicted to last only until her 15th birthday, but Joe and Linda's dedication added, with a team of other helpers, a further ten years to Lisa's life. Marian and I love Joe and Linda to bits, they're like a real brother and sister!

There are many, many more incidents from true life that I was going to write about, but I'll finish with these little ditties – whilst in Australia.

We stayed at a University complex in Melbourne, when staying in Youth Hostel Accommodation. From the University campus (closed because of their semester or holiday period) we journeyed through to Ballarat, the Gold Mining centre, complete with Olde Worlde charm gold mining activities. We could even go 'panning for gold' with obviously grains of brass filings that were put into a sluice, with water running down to the small creek (man-made of course) with people acting in '150-years-ago-costumes' of the gold mining town, a complete settlement in that era.

We journeyed on to Adelaide with a sleepover in a small village about 20 kilometres from the city of Adelaide, where Joe met us at the bus station. We were taken to a suburb of Adelaide, a village called Durnan Court, and we stayed at a University Lecturer's single storey house complete with small chandeliers, a washroom, and another wet-room with another toilet facility. All good, thus far. I switched on the air conditioning – big mistake! Why? Because we could see electrical sparks arcing and sparking slowly up the wall from the electrical cable.

"It's a death trap!" shouts out my youngest daughter Kathleen.

"Don't be silly," I replied and rang my phone to contact Joe, turning off the electricity beforehand. Joe dutifully arrived and sorted it out himself.

Two more incidents quickly followed. During that night, there was an electrical storm, thunder and lightning, but strange as it may seem with the absence of rain. The next day, our Kathleen goes walkabout, and gets followed home by an Australian cattle dog – a Blue Heeler, Staffie cross.

"There's a dangerous dog following me Dad," says she.

"Oh," says I, "we'd better get it sorted," says I, wearily. The only danger that stupid mutt posed was the fact it could literally lick you to death, the animal had a lovely nature and, in our lounge, would lie on its back with its paws in the air, waiting to have its tummy tickled.

We kept the animal for three whole days, where it became one of the family. With great reluctance, we had to say g'day and g'd bye to our four-legged Aussie Blue Heeler and then we had to ring the Aussie equivalent of the English RSPCA which we contacted.

The last incident, same house, different day, at Durnan Court, was the water leak. One of the sink basins in the wet room, which had a shower, also had facilities for hanging up wet clothing, to allow them to 'drip-dry'. The cold-water tap started to leak in the connecting pipework. Easy-peasy, thinks I, I'll just 'tweak' the pipework - and cure the leak. Wrong. I inadvertently 'strangled' the pipe and quickly asked one of the Aussie neighbours as to the whereabouts of the stopcock. After switching off the water supply, Joe dutifully arrived once again, and sorted it out.

# The Final Chapter

## *Biting the Bullet*

My life has been amazing and, don't you know, I would relive that life all over again – if I had to.

What? Undergo the mental torture of being constantly reminded of those humble beginnings of *rejection*? Yes, even that. The point is, to succeed in this life one has to 'toughen up', to be a man, sometimes.

I'm reminded of that Johnny Cash song, 'A Boy Named Sue', when, after numerous times of having to live down the many years of mental anguish because of 'that name', of a feminine name of Sue, the son in question literally had to fight, by fist-fighting his way in life. The son decides to go looking for this swine of a father who had put him through all this aggro, and they finally meet up.

With a 'kick and a gauging' type of fist-fight with his paternal father, he asks of him, "Why did you give me the name of Sue?" Indeed, finally, they do achieve a real father/son relationship, don't they?

Me, I had to grasp the nettle, to forget about my shortcomings, forget about the tears of abject sorrow, when, as a young lad of eight years old and onwards, I'd cry myself to sleep. Because of who I was, I would be constantly reminded during my formative years by my Nana of the circumstances of my birth. It was during those times I would grow to hate her – yes, hate her – for the mental torture she would put me through.

You see, I was a 'rebel' in every sense of the word. I'd 'back-answer' her; she would 'work the sword in' so to speak, knowing the hurt she could inflict when I refused to pander to her every whim, when I refused to do her bidding.

She wanted to control me - but I wouldn't let her. She had met her match. I was now her equal, and what's more, she knew it. Big boys, dear reader, don't cry, do they? Oh yes, they do!

'Sticks and stones may break my bones, but words will never hurt me' as the saying goes. Do words hurt? Yes, dear reader, words indeed do hurt. I never, ever, let her, or anyone else for that matter, see my tears. However, in the solitude of my bedroom, with the covers pulled over my head, I would unashamedly let the tears flow. You see, tears are a release.

I just had to BITE THE BULLET, as the saying goes, take my life by the horns and be a man, albeit a man who, from time to time, sheds tears.

I was given the name of Bettenson because it was my mother's married name. I've cried tears of anguish of why oh why could this soldier boy not have been my father. I just had to BITE THE BULLET, and because it was an emotional rollercoaster, take life as it is and deal with things at face value.

I have the last picture postcard my mother Amy was sent, and was to read, and the poignant reminder of his last written words of a loving husband. I will not, ever, highlight those words in print. Suffice it to say, when Caroline my eldest daughter came with me to the War Memorial in Lake, also my grand-daughter Annabelle, came too. Just to re-cap, three months into my mum's pregnancy, her mother Kathleen Louisa died, aged 43. This was in 1942. A shock indeed for my poor mother.

Eventually, a total reject by the name of John Brian Bettenson, was born. 'Bootsie' had arrived on the world's stage, on the canvas of life. This was on New Year's Day, 1943.

*The ending of a relationship* – I had to think long and hard as to whether or not I should include the next few items in my book. After due consideration, I decided to include them anyway.

One Saturday I went to work my four hours overtime, then came home, ready to relax and decide what to do for the remainder of the weekend.

"By the way John, your relationship with that girlfriend of yours is over, as she came over to see you early this morning. You can't afford a girlfriend on your wages, and besides, you need to concentrate on your apprenticeship," says Nan.

"You've what?" I exploded. "You've sent her packing! What right have you to interfere in my private life?"

"It's for the best John, she'll get over it, it really is for the best. Come on, I've prepared a nice dinner in the oven for you. I'll get it out for you, I expect you're hungry, aren't you?"

"Stuff you," I shouted at her, "and you can stick your dinner where the sun can't shine. I'm off to try and rectify the damage you've caused to my relationship with Marian. I love her, Nan, and one day I'm going to marry her. You can stick that in your pipe and smoke it."

With that, I stormed out of the house and to attempt some damage limitation, I went up, on foot, to try and smooth things over with Marian. This is how controlling my step-gran really was. She always had to call the shots, she really did.

*Teaching me a lesson* – One day, when I was 17 years old, my grandfather called for me to come downstairs as he had something to say to me – in the kitchen.

"Okay, Grandad," I shouted down to him, "just coming." I could tell from the look on his face he was not a happy bunny.

"Right, young fellow my lad, I'm going to teach you a lesson you won't forget in a hurry."

With that, he went to the back door of the kitchen, locked it and pocketed the key. Next, he produced a second key and locked the second door leading out of the kitchen to the rest of the house, leaving the key in the lock.

He then proceeded to undo his belt buckle. Now, casting my mind back to the Cottage Homes where I stayed for about a year and a bit, brought back memories of an incident where I was bullied.

I was about six and half years old at the time and three boys got hold of me, and as two boys held me tight, the third, who was holding a powerful magnifying glass, trained it on the back of my left hand. That pinpoint of light from the sun's rays made me scream out in agony, before they let me go, laughing at me as they cleared off. I made a vow on that day that *nobody* would ever get the better of me ever again.

Sadly, that day with grandfather wishing to give me a good hiding with a two-inch wide leather belt, had now come. When both of his hands were preoccupied with the undoing of the brass buckle, without thinking, I whacked him just below his left eye. I hit him sufficiently hard enough to knock him off his feet and he collapsed in a heap on the floor. I calmly walked to the door with the key still in the lock and opened the door and went out of the house. I was immediately sorry for what I'd done but *she* had put him up to it, *she* was the one who'd loaded the gun, for poor old grandad to fire the bullets. He sustained a black-eye, of sorts, what we would term a 'mouse' under his left eye, much to the amusement of his fellow workmates apparently.

*The Final Straw* – the last incident was the proverbial straw that broke the camel's back. Once again, Nan had a right cob on. She was screaming the 'B' word at me, the one ending in 'd', referring to my illegitimacy. She was like a screaming banshee, completely out of control. I was in the front room at the time, she was in the lounge. She would scream abuse at me, with the lounge door partly open, then abruptly close it. A few seconds later, she would come out with a few more verbal obscenities. Gradually, I began to simmer with rage, and as time went on began to really get annoyed. I was like a pressure cooker, ready to explode.

Finally, I decided on a course of action. In the front room, on the mantlepiece, stood a beautiful glass vase. Its colour was the colour of jade, a lovely ornament, to say the least, and expensive too. If she keeps this up, I'm going to 'let fly' with this ornament, I decided.

She did keep up the non-stop tirade, and I indeed 'let fly' with this vase and threw it in her direction, whereupon it shattered against the top of the door that protected her from receiving a direct hit.

Silence then finally terminated even Nan's outbursts, as for once she was completely lost for words. Most probably I'd put the fear of God into her, and I left the house to have a few lager shandies to bury my sorrows.

The following day, in the late afternoon, two officers of the law, a police constable and a police woman, kindly informed me that I had two hours in which to pack up my things and leave.

This chapter in my life was now over, and in a way, I was only too glad to leave the house, with all the shenanigans that were an ongoing pain in the butt, as far as I was concerned.

I got out my bicycle, and balancing my suitcase on the crossbar with what other few bags I could safely carry draped around the handlebars, I made my way up to my girlfriend's house. Initially, I only asked to stay the night, but Marian's mum said to me I could stay there as a lodger, as long as I paid my way, which is what I did.

When, at the age of 23 years, I gave my heart to the Lord Jesus Christ, HE became my Lord and Saviour and was to become the new father figure in my life.

UNASHAMEDLY, I wept my way to Calvery. You see, Jeshua (Jesus) the Son of God, had just triumphed over the grave and I had now become by God's Grace, a child of the living God. I knew it, in my heart, I had been born again, of the Spirit of God *John 3:3*

We are heirs of the Father, Joint-heirs of the Son, we are 'children' of the Kingdom, we are, we are one in Christ Jesus. *Romans 8:16 and 17*

For God so loved the world, that He gave his only begotten Son, that whosoever believeth in Him, should not perish but have eternal life. *John 3:16*

My Father, in heaven's rich glory, had now filled the void, the emptiness, of a life devoid of the love of two parents. My mother, every time she came on a visit, every single time she met up with Nan, would return back to her hostel to become a broken woman again, until she remarried.

I simply had to Bite the Bullet - I was a fitter called Bootsie, a true Isle of Wighter.

Yes, Bootsie, you've bitten the bullet, and I can only hope, dear reader, you've enjoyed my journey through the pathway of life, even through the tears of sorrow as well as joy.

It is now 7 o'clock in the evening here in Oakfield where I live at this moment in time. Shortly, my wife and I hope to move to a three-bedroom bungalow in Binstead, God willing. The move could take place, should everything fall into line, by December, during the first week, in 2020. I'm not counting my chickens however until contracts for the aforesaid sale have been exchanged and signed.

It's tipping it down with rain outside and any sorting out of the contents of the sheds in my garden have to be put on hold. My wife, bless her, has decided because it is now so close to the onset of Winter, to pack all our summer clothes into packing cases indoors, or indeed into large suitcases that were used for going abroad with. At the last count, it was the fourth time, to visit Marian's relatives in Adelaide, South Australia.

There are a few things I'd forgotten to mention after we made our move from Oaklawn, Wootton, to the Curator's Lodge in Fairlee Cemetery. My grandfather also took charge of the Halberry Lane cemetery close to the Mountbatten hospice.

It was whilst I was living there, that I had a run-in with five other lads of my own age. They were David or Dick H., Chris G., Nigel T., Malcolm P. and on occasion, Roger C., one of two brothers who lived in the same lane at the 'H.P. House' near Binfield Corner at the end of Fairlee Road.

After explaining pleasantries and introducing ourselves, Dick H. decided to test my wrestling ability, by suddenly grabbing hold of me by the neck and holding me in a tight grip. Suffice it to say, I did manage to hold my own with him and got out of the choke-hold he had me under, much to the bemusement of the others looking on.

Obviously, they all wanted to know if I had the guts to stand up for myself, and to be honest, no punches were thrown or any kicking involved. We both shook hands after that initial skirmish and forever after became firm friends.

I was thirteen and a half years old at the time, and every Saturday afternoon the 'wrestling' was on the telly. The stars were 'Jackie T.V. Pallo', Mick McManus and 'Giant Haystacks', who died after a bout with 'The Big Daddy' when Big Daddy executed what he himself called 'the Splash. This is when 24-stone Big Daddy would 'splash' down on his opponent by throwing his whole body weight face downward onto his opponent. In this case, it was Giant Haystacks. No contest, Big Daddy was three or four stones heavier than Giant Haystacks, eventually resulting in Giant Haystack's death.

Then there was 'Billy Two Rivers' with his famous 'Tomahawk Chop', when after being thrown all over the auction by his opponent, Two Rivers would then wake up out of his stupor, beat ten bales of sugar out of the floor, then do his spectacular war dance and annihilate the opposition – with his famous 'Tomahawk Chop. All very good stuff.

Then there was 'Kendo' Nagasaki, the martial arts expert turned wrestler. He sported a Samurai type facemask, laced up behind his head, which was shaven except for a top-knot that was left to grow from the top of his head, in the centre of a tattooed five pointed star. Allowances were made in the construction of the mask to allow the top-knot or ponytail type of hair, to protrude from the central part of the helmet.

He was never, ever beaten in the ring, and when he did retire from wrestling, he had an 'unveiling' ceremony to reveal his face, free at last from the Samurai mask – all good stuff really.

Kendo used to be a nasty piece of work and in nine times out of ten would knock his opponent out. We teenage lads aged 13½ to 15½ years old, would practice the various moves that the wrestlers would use, except forearm smashes, by Mick McManus and the like; the half Nelson, full Nelson, hip throws, full body scissors and even the straight-armed lift. This is when your opponent's arm is locked against the joint, and then the arm is used to lift up the body of one's opponent. It was good clean fun. To say that at that age up until the time I met my future wife-to-be, when I was 18 years old, is an understatement.

I've never gone looking for trouble, but if trouble found me, then so be it.

1. Rules of Conduct – okay, there are none (Queensbury Rules E.T.)
2. Never show fear
3. If you're going to do it, do it first
4. Never tell one's opponent what you intend to do

One night I was working nightshift, when the latest craze (even with grown-up men we can act like schoolchildren) was to assault one another from a water-filled squeegee bottle and things started to get a little out of hand. One of the lads, who was absolutely brilliant with his accuracy using a squeegee bottle, got me good and proper when I was due to leave in the wee small hours of the morning, on a half-night lieu night (equivalent to a half day's holiday, of which we had a half a dozen or so allocated to us).

Unbeknown to me, knowing I was finishing my shift early, he went outside the Union Jack Flag where we parked our cars off-road, and waited for me to get into my car, outside Columbine. It was in the middle of summer, so my window was wound down.

As soon as I'd used my seat belt to belt up, clunk clicked and all that, he emptied the contents of the squeegee bottle all down my neck and back. I was absolutely soaked. To him it was a big joke. Me, I was absolutely beside myself with pure unadulterated rage, but I just had to grin and bear it and had to drive home, absolutely drenched.

The next night, whilst driving to work, I began to simmer. By the time I'd arrived at work, I'd worked up a right old head of steam – I was out for blood – revenge. After clocking in, I went straight to the tool store assigned to our department and selected the largest torque wrench in the tool kit.

Then, although I shouldn't have done this, I did give him fair warning that I was armed with a very heavy torque wrench and meant business! Pound for pound, he weighed in at 18 stone. He was about 6'4" tall and an ex-bouncer, to boot. I weighed about 10st 10lbs.

"You come near me with that stupid water bottle, and I swear to God I'll take your bloomin' head off your shoulders," I shouted at him.

"Have you got it pal?" I said.

Bob Downer (my other workmate on the Shorts wing) says, "Calm down Bootsie, let it go mate."

"As long as he understands where I'm coming from, I'll be fine Bob, ok?"

From that night onwards, the water bottles disappeared and normality, once again, returned to the shop floor. The chargehand at that time sorted the situation out. He went by the name of Ian Muncaster. He's dead and gone now. He was a very quiet and unassuming person really, a gentleman in fact, and quite young when he died.

To be honest, quite a few chargehands and foremen have died while working for GKN. They are expected to eat, drink, sleep, work for GKN. Although they are paid handsomely, they are expected to literally devote every minute of their time, should their bosses desire it. They may all live in fine houses and live in the lap of luxury – but is it worth it? Not for me it wouldn't be, but there by God's Grace go I.

In the summer of 1958, a year before I left school, I got a part-time job during the school holidays. I worked at Little Fairlee Farm, owned by Farmer Bradley and his wife Felicity.

It was fun working on the farm, and one of the incidents that came to mind was the Victoria plum incident. Just at the entrance to the new Farm Cottage, stood a Victoria plum tree. The plums on that tree were everywhere. The long hot summer and heavy showers of rain produced a bumper crop of Victoria plums.

113

Now another young farm hand, Frank C., worked at the farm also. Unfortunately, Frank had a problem, he was blind in one eye. Farmer Bradley used to act like a young school kid at times and would get in on the act. He and Frank, the other lad, armed themselves and started throwing overripe Victoria plums that littered the ground among the trees, at each other. One well aimed squelchy plum hit Frank in his one remaining eye that he *could* see out of. This completely blinded him and he became incandescent with rage. Frank then went to the deep-litter shed, which houses the factory hens, and also some caged birds.

Frank had approximately two dozen eggs he stockpiled in four six-pack egg cartons, went up to the barn opposite the hen house – and lay in wait for Farmer Bradley.

"Frank, where the hell are you?" says Farmer Bradley. "I'm still paying you to work you know."

As he drew closer to the deep-litter shed which housed the chickens, he came into range where the young farmhand, Frank, was lying in wait.

Splat! The first egg struck the farmer fair and square on his tweed hacking jacket, swiftly followed by the second, third and fourth – which were all pretty much on target. I was in the hen house watching this one-way battle waged by young Frank. The next egg was a corker. It struck Farmer Bradley right on the peak of his flat-cap and dripped down his face. He shook his head and quickly retreated back the way he'd come, the eggs now being thrown with gay abandon, some of which were still hitting their target.

Frank had wreaked his revenge for the blindness he'd suffered from the Victoria plum incident.

Now to the next incident, involving William, the pedigree bull. It so happened that the Bradleys purchased a pedigree bull calf, to rear and eventually to breed from. Whilst the bull was growing up, it was as tame as could be, in fact the farmer could as often as not be seen riding the bull around the farmyard. Eventually the bull reached maturity and was still soft natured and was allowed to be in a field adjacent to the main part of the farmyard. However, on the day in question, a few young heifers had strayed into the field at the bottom of the meadow, when the bull spots the head cowman marching towards the young cows to shut them in another field.

William the Bull suddenly changes from a tame, soft matured animal, into a very angry bull, just like that. He starts to paw the earth, then sets off, gradually building up a right head of steam. Just as the bull was about to attack the young farmhand, Farmer Bradley on his Massey Ferguson tractor, drove between the bull and his experienced cowhand, just in the nick of time and without a moment too soon. I believe he would have been 'brown bread' but for Farmer Bradley's timely intervention.

After that, poor William had his nose pierced and was kept tethered by a rope through his nose piercing.

What never ceased to amaze me was the milking scenario, when each cow went to its own allocated part of the dairy. The best 'milker' of his herd was a beautiful shaped animal called 'Snowdrop'. I don't know why, but one day she kicked out sideways and caught Farmer Bradley on the thigh muscle of his right leg, which suffered a bloomin' great bruise, which began to display a colourful display on that leg.

What did Farmer Bradley do? He went out and decided to teach Snowdrop a lesson, with the aid of a swishy stick. From that day onwards, he couldn't get anywhere near her as she was out for blood. The only person who could milk her and place the suction cups of the milking gear on her teats was a young schoolgirl by the name of Mary B. (the daughter of a friend of the family).

Farmer Bradley was a good man, and it was out of character for him to react at the time to being badly kicked in the thigh. Immediately Snowdrop kicked him, Farmer Bradley decided she was going to pay in the manner I've described above.

I would have loved to work on the land, as a farmer, but a skilled man's pay in industry is far more rewarding than working on the land. You didn't go to grammar school to end up as a farmer John, was my grandfather and surrogate partner's wish, as I neared the end of my schooling. No, their wish was for me to become an apprentice and ultimately becoming a skilled Apprenticed Fitter on Board/come Engineer. It was a great way of earning a living.

\*\*\*

**Note bene (NB)**

Well, that's all for now folks.  I hope you've enjoyed my journey through the pathway of life.  Who knows, there may even be a sequel!

Take care!

Bootsie Bettenson

Printed in Great Britain
by Amazon

74187567R00071